Praise for *How to Be Exceptional*

"This book offers compelling evidence that growing one's strengths leads to greater results. However, it takes it to the next level by teaching how those identified strengths can be developed to an even greater degree to distinguish you from the crowd. This book is a must-read for anyone wanting to positively stand out in an organization or for leaders wanting to raise the overall performance of the organization."

—Cindy Brinkley, Vice President,
Global Human Resources, General Motors

"*How to Be Exceptional* is the best book on professional development I have read in decades. It reinforces the emerging wisdom that the path to greatness is really about building profound strengths, rather than through relentlessly focusing on one's weaknesses. But, the real value of this important book is the wealth of practical advice it offers on assessing strengths and developing them. This is a great road map for leaders seeking to optimize their growth and impact."

—Michael A. Peel, Yale University, Vice President,
Human Resources and Administration

"The work of the authors of this book has proven helpful in filling the gap from inspirational to practical "how to" realities of leadership improvement. The difference is an unusual blend of credible and uncompromising research married with years of successful application with leaders and organizations. . . . My encouragement to readers . . . dive into this book, choose an area that matters, and go for exceptional."

—Kevin D. Wilde, VP, Organization Effectiveness and
Chief Learning Officer, General Mills, author of
Dancing with the Talent Stars: 25 Moves That Matter Now

"Zenger Folkman's research and tools have provided excellent guidance to leaders I've worked with over the years. The tools allowed them to create actionable goals and inspired them to actively pursue excellence in leadership. The findings related to companion behaviors is exciting. It enhances what's been presented in prior books and makes extraordinary leadership seem like an achievable goal. I would recommend this book to anyone committed to the journey."

—Pam Mabry, Director, Human Resources,
The Boeing Company

"The Zenger Folkman organization has had a profound effect on leadership development. Their research reveals the impact of strengths-based development on individual and organization success across industries and geographies. Their competency model and 360 evaluation provide the framework around which to build a development plan. *How to Be Exceptional* goes a step further by providing a clear, practical approach to framing a development plan and going about making it happen."

"The authors have hit on the next evolution of focusing on strengths. They've utilized compelling research to understand what it takes to become an exceptional leader. The insightful tools and developmental approaches help address fatal flaws and push your existing strengths over the edge to exceptional."

"*How to Be Exceptional* shines much-needed light on a topic that is littered with self-help books, motivational programs, and fads. It cuts through this clutter with a path that is straightforward and, even better, entirely based on statistically based evidence. The authors take the groundbreaking concept of driving leadership effectiveness by building our strengths to a whole new level of practical implementation, providing us with a brilliantly clear road map. I have found this body of work to be absolutely invaluable to my organization and to me personally. I cannot imagine a person in a leadership role today who would not find value from reading this book cover to cover."

"My organization has benefited for years from Zenger Folkman's involvement in our Leadership Training Programs, which are based on the principles included in this book. We have seen that people are much more successful when we focus on improving their natural leadership strengths while minimizing their weaknesses. I believe this is a must-read for executives interested in truly improving leadership within their organizations!"

"*How to Be Exceptional* is a breakthrough milestone in the emerging business case for evidence-based management. Building on two decades of earlier research, the authors brilliantly lay out a simple, concrete, scientifically validated model for achieving consistently superior business results through leadership. This isn't a bunch of academic gobbledygook that sounds convincing but can't be executed. To the contrary, its magic is its simplicity, pragmatism, and focus. It is an easy-to-follow formula for dramatically improving one's success in business."

—Eric Severson, Senior Vice President, Talent, Gap Inc.

"*How to Be Exceptional* demystifies the leadership quest that so many individuals and organizations pursue. It avoids the simplistic cookie-cutter approaches that never inspired anyone, and it avoids the dogma of leadership that never seems to explain exactly *how* to become an amazing leader. This book provides the necessary guidance for developing extraordinary strengths while still enabling a unique leadership journey. Becoming exceptional is possible for all willing to follow this deeply rich guide and improve upon their greatest passions."

—Sandra Hunter, Sr. Director of Leadership and
Employee Development, Symantec Corporation

"Leadership development too often has been defined as fixing weaknesses and becoming better in those competencies that the leader performs below average. This book clearly shows how building strengths makes the difference both for the leader and the organization. It gives actionable advice about shifting the focus from fixing weaknesses to building strengths and gaining exceptional business outcomes, along with an innovative methodology for strength development.

"It gives business leaders and leadership development managers the insights, pathways, and methodologies to actually create great leadership and deliver winning results."

—Pablo Riera, Chairman, Grupo P&A

"Each year brings greater competition and complexity in our business, and exceptional leadership is the equalizer. The authors have put forward another highly practical, research-supported tool kit for leaders at every level. Accelerated success springs from leveraging our greatest strengths and adding more. If you want to take your game or your teams to an exceptional level, read on!"

—John Farrell, Organizational Development Director,
Marathon Oil Company

"So much that has been written in recent years about 'discovering your strengths' rarely extends beyond the notional or platitudinous, that it is refreshing to be immersed in real research on leadership effectiveness that shows its *tangible* impact. The authors create a compelling case for lifting leadership effectiveness from the (somewhat pejorative) realm of 'soft skills' to a plane that equates these competencies with 'harder' disciplines in two ways: not only can these skills be learned, but they can have a similar impact on bottom-line results and employee performance. Leadership cross-training is an approach that can have a powerful impact on helping good leaders become exceptional ones."

—Jaime Gonzales, Head of Professional Development,
Jet Propulsion Laboratory

"Zenger and Folkman amaze us again by demonstrating, based on their extensive research that: 'leaders are not perfect' but become exceptional by developing their unique and profound strengths. This in turn skyrockets employee productivity, customer loyalty, and sustainable financial performance."

—Rodolfo Gallegos, Emeritus VP of HR,
Kellogg, Gillette, and Holcim Corporations;
currently lectures on HR management
and leadership development
and serves as an executive coach

"Zenger and Folkman's first book, *The Extraordinary Leader*, demonstrated the importance of building strengths, and after utilizing their groundbreaking approach with clients all over the world, they now have collected clear evidence that the approach works."

—Kimo Kippen, Chief Learning Officer, Hilton Worldwide

"This must-read book challenges the way we perceived leadership developmental plans. Outstanding leaders are not perfect but focus on developing a few distinctive strengths.

"The impact of this approach creates a very positive context in which leaders are eager to identify strategies and work on developing distinctive strengths to become exceptional."

—Isabelle Champagne, Director, Training and
Organizational Development, Transat A.T. Inc.

HOW TO BE
EXCEPTIONAL

DRIVE LEADERSHIP SUCCESS
BY MAGNIFYING
YOUR STRENGTHS

JOHN H. ZENGER, JOSEPH R. FOLKMAN,
ROBERT H. SHERWIN, JR., BARBARA A. STEEL

NEW YORK   CHICAGO   SAN FRANCISCO
LISBON   LONDON   MADRID   MEXICO CITY   MILAN
NEW DELHI   SAN JUAN   SEOUL   SINGAPORE
SYDNEY   TORONTO

6 7 8 9 10   DOC/DOC   1 8 7 6 5 4

ISBN 978-0-07-179148-9
MHID 0-07-179148-5

e-ISBN 978-0-07-179149-6
e-MHID 0-07-179149-3

Library of Congress Cataloging-in-Publication Data

How to be exceptional : drive leadership success by magnifying your strengths / by John Zenger ... [et al.].
   p. cm.
   ISBN 978-0-07-179148-9 (alk. paper) — ISBN 0-07-179148-5 (alk. paper)
1. Leadership.   2. Executive ability.   I. Zenger, John. H.
   HD57.7.H684   2013
   658.4'092—dc23

                                                          2012016230

McGraw-Hill books are available at special quantity discounts to use as premiums and sales promotions or for use in corporate training programs. To contact a representative, please e-mail us at bulksales@mcgraw-hill.com.

Contents

——————| PART I

**What Leaders Can Learn
from Their Strengths**

————————————

PART II

How Exceptional
Strengths Are Developed

Foreword

At last count, there are over 91,000 leadership books on Amazon .com, and I found a similar number of training programs with a recent online search. That's encouraging and overwhelming. Encouraging, as effective leadership today is more important than ever before. Overwhelming as a leadership development practitioner, because I am expected to keep up with the latest thinking. So I read as much as I can, listen to as many speakers on the topic as possible, and keep an observant eye on what most makes a difference.

What I've found is that there is no shortage of theories, historical figures, metaphorical models, and attribute lists. A sample of the leadership books by historical figures includes lessons from Machiavelli, Lincoln, Gandhi, and Attila the Hun. The metaphorical views portray leadership as an engine, jazz, poetry, war, a bus, and a rock. Finally, there is a logical series of the rules of leadership as a list, with books counting down from "417 rules of awesomely bold leadership" all the way down to the one rule of leadership. Furthermore, there is a new book right around the corner from the latest sports champ, the current Wall Street darling, and the hot new management guru. All in all, more than a bit confusing for someone trying to help leaders grow in a rational and sustainable way.

For years I've had the good fortune to work for organizations and leaders who set the bar high for performance and growth, fueled by the external demands for "more" and the internal drive for "better." However, as a development professional for more than 30 years, I was often at a loss to provide credible and useful resources to address this need. The theories, history lessons, and metaphors only go so far.

These past few years, the work of the authors of this book has proven helpful in filling the gap from inspirational to practical "how to" realities of leadership improvement. The difference is an unusual blend of credible and uncompromising research married with years of successful application with leaders and organizations. The result is innovative, at times challenging conventional wisdom, and ultimately useful. I have seen talent in my organization engage and improve based on this work.

This book addresses the key questions my leaders often pose when trying to improve, including:

- What do I need to work on that would really make a difference?
- Is it more important to fix a weakness or build a strength?
- I've tried to get better and nothing seems to work. Now what?

When we first considered using the "how to be extraordinary" approach, I had to answer a few questions from the CEO. I remember his skepticism over why the next round of top leadership training should concentrate on strength building versus obsessing over minor weaknesses. While acknowledging some need to concentrate on what the authors call fatal flaws, I replied that most of our leaders would be wasting their time making small, incremental improvements on a few, below-average scores that may not matter in the long run. Besides, I said, if we concentrate all our efforts getting everyone to average, that is what we will achieve—a company of average leaders.

We agreed that we needed more exceptional leaders with profound strengths that matter.

And that's my encouragement to readers now. Dive into this book, choose an area that matters, and go for exceptional.

—Kevin D. Wilde, VP, Organization Effectiveness and
Chief Learning Officer, General Mills,
Author of *Dancing with the Talent Stars:*
25 Moves That Matter Now

Acknowledgments

We wish to acknowledge our energetic group of colleagues who collectively lift leadership development to new levels. They are:

Andrea Templeman	Kerri Price
Angela Bass	Lynn Nicholson
BreAnne Okoren	Mark Brown
Brett Savage	Matthew Bentz
Christopher Evans	Michael McDonald
Damon Argyle	Mikel Dover
Denise Dalton	Natasha Beach
Gregory Johnson	Pamela Kemp
Jill Mancini	Daniel Orcutt
Karen Williams	Terry Robert
Kathleen Stinnett	Thomas Harker
Kelly Clayton	Traci Consolini

We dedicate this book to our many global partners who have banded with us to bring strengths-based leadership development to the world. It is truly a noble and rewarding cause.

Be Great
· San Francisco, USA

CBE
· Amsterdam, The Netherlands
· Mumbai, India
· Maputo, Mozambique
· Ho Chi Minh City, Vietnam

CENDE
· Mexico City, Mexico

The CLEMMER Group
· Toronto, Canada

Extraordinary Performance
· Toronto, Canada

Grupo P&A
· Campinas and São Paulo, Brazil
· Vigo, Spain
· Lisbon, Portugal

HPI
· Bogotá, Columbia
· Quito, Ecuador

IOCAP
· Milano, Italy

KeyLogic
· Beijing, Guangzhou, Shanghai, and Shenzen, China

Louis Allen Southern Africa
· Johannesburg, South Africa

Natural Direction
· London, United Kingdom

OHTEN Group
· London, United Kingdom

rogenSi
· Sydney and Melbourne, Australia
· London, United Kingdom
· New York, USA
· Hong Kong
· Auckland, New Zealand
· Singapore
· Dubai, United Arab Emirates

Skills Worldwide
· Cairo, Egypt
· Dubai, United Arab Emirates

SmartWorks
· Tokyo, Japan

Introduction

Like a gigantic pendulum swinging, there has been a dramatic shift in the world of leadership development. We have moved from a focus on fixing weaknesses all the way over to a focus on building strengths. Without question, it is the most profound change in this realm to occur in the past 50 years. While the idea was talked about by Peter Drucker in 1967, it has only been in the past five years that it has taken hold. We strongly doubt that the pendulum will ever swing back. There is too much good research supporting the fundamentals that underlie this shift in thinking.

The emphasis to date, however, has been on *discovering* strengths. This is an obvious and extremely logical beginning step. Books have been written about the importance of understanding your personal strengths and then employing those existing strengths to your advantage. These books and articles have focused largely on the various tools and techniques for identifying one's strengths. These range from self-assessment instruments with as many as 240 items to much simpler, briefer questionnaires. Some would argue that it is rare for individuals to be truly capable of seeing either their strengths or their weaknesses. We would fall in that camp because of our extensive work with 360-degree feedback instruments. Self-scores are not highly correlated with the collective opinions of those who work around a person on a regular basis. Nor are most leadership self-assessments highly predictive of those leaders' business results.

Why This Book?

It is one thing to ferret out the things you are good at doing. Making that discovery is obviously of great value. But now what? It is nice to know what you are reasonably good at doing. The bigger question is how you can dramatically improve that skill or competence so that it truly becomes one of your signature strengths. Why? Because there is a huge mound of data that proves that it is the people who have profound strengths who produce the best results. The more such strengths they have, the better the results. We've found in our research that there is a huge incentive for leaders to develop three to five traits, behaviors, or competencies (call them what you will) so that these strengths are at the 90th percentile in comparison with the rankings for other leaders. When that happens, both the leader and the leader's organization truly flourish.

But like Sisyphus pushing the rock up the hill, only to have it roll back, many leaders do not know how to transform something they do reasonably well into something that is truly exceptional. If it were easy, they would have started doing it. If they knew exactly what to do, they would have been well into doing it.

For example, let's use a common target for leadership development. In reviewing thousands of development plans for leaders, we find that becoming a better listener is a frequently selected target. Doing a few reasonably obvious things propels you to the 75th percentile on listening skills, when comparing you with others. These would include things like "Stop talking" or "Don't interrupt others when they are speaking." Getting your behavior up to a "B" level is reasonably easy. But moving from this being a B in your list of leadership behaviors up to being a solid A is more challenging. Some well-intentioned colleague might suggest, "Take a class" or "Read a book." But the leader who aspires to become a better listener will often respond with, "I've taken that class" or "I've read that book." Now what?

Moving from the 75th to the 90th percentile is a formidable challenge for most leaders. This is the hardest part of the climb because the obvious things have been done. The logical, intuitive actions have all been tried. Furthermore, is building a strength simply a continuation of the same things that you did to acquire the basic skill? Or are there more effective ways to develop that B behavior into an A?

What This Book Is About

This book picks up where others leave off. Yes, we'll talk about how you can determine what your strengths are, but we won't stop there. Instead, this is all about ways by which you can take the strengths you identify and develop them into ones that truly distinguish you and enable you to make the highest contribution to your organization.

We begin our book by providing some compelling evidence that leaders with three to five skills at the 90th percentile indeed make a gargantuan impact on their organizations. If you correlate these leaders' perceived effectiveness with employee engagement, customer satisfaction, productivity, profitability, or retention of employees—in fact, with virtually every quantifiable business outcome you can imagine—you'll find a strong connection.

Once we make that case, our next step will be to provide some additional data designed to convince you that these exceptional leaders attain their standing for one, and only one, reason. It is not because they are perfect, nor are they moderately good at everything. In their roles as leaders, they are really outstanding at doing a few things well.

We'll make a quick detour to assure you that you are not wasting time if you work on your weaknesses. Visible, blatant weaknesses invariably detract. Fixing these flat sides helps, but it does not negate the immutable law that says "Fixing weaknesses never made anyone exceptional."

A Second Huge Shift in Mindset

We tenaciously make the case that strengths can be developed. It happens in different ways from merely acquiring the rudiments of a skill. But strengths can be developed. Many writers on this topic today would argue that you should discover one or two strengths and then work hard to use them and protect them. They contend that strengths are not amenable to all that much change.

Psychologists have labeled some human characteristics as talents. These talents are somewhat hardwired into you at a very early stage. Try to teach someone to have perfect pitch after he or she is eight years of age and you will not have much success. Yet children at an earlier age can frequently learn this skill. Blow a puff of air into a child's face and time how long it takes the child to blink. Little can be done to make that response faster.

We have accumulated extensive data that show people making significant progress in their leadership skills, and that leads us to the most powerful message of the book and the one we hope you won't miss. Developing strengths isn't the same thing as fixing weaknesses. Indeed, there are several different pathways to building your strengths.

Leadership Cross-Training—the Third Big Idea

The message we don't want you to miss is the concept that the same principles that apply to developing some physical attributes and skills can be applied to acquiring leadership skills. The idea is simple. Just as athletes engage in cross-training, and for precisely the same reasons, leaders can use cross-training to take a B competency and develop it into an A. Athletes don't use cross-training as a way to learn the basics of a skill. Nor do they use cross-training to move into an intermediate level of performance. It's when they aspire to really excel that they engage in a series of activities that have been shown to be highly correlated with the skill they seek to build. For example, a long-distance runner who is very good but trying to get to the world-class level might employ various kinds of cross-training programs. A recent article in *Runner's World* magazine suggested runners apply "Wet Equity" as a cross-training idea. The author noted that runners can increase their fitness, strength, and flexibility through various aerobic swimming exercises in a pool, a workout regimen for runners that simultaneously supports injury prevention and recovery.

As with athletic cross-training, we have amassed strong statistical evidence that for every leadership competency, there are behaviors that have a statistically significant link to that target leadership skill. Many of our colleagues have suggested that this may well be the most valuable contribution that our research has made to the practice of leadership development.

Many Paths for Developing Strengths

The good news is that there are many pathways for strengths development in addition to the powerful technique of cross-training. The second part of the book takes a broad, encompassing view of how someone might first go about choosing a skill or competency to work on. We suggest several criteria to assist in making this decision. We then describe different procedures to use in developing a strength, including the basic steps we all use when learning a new skill, the indispensable role of feedback in developing strengths, the many ways to build learning and development into the warp and woof of the job, and the steps we can take to make this all more sustainable.

Further Thoughts on the Strengths Movement

We obviously have strong feelings about the importance of focusing on strengths, and we cannot resist elaborating on this as the most effective personal development approach. As such, this doesn't just apply to the people with *vice president, director, manager,* or *supervisor* by their name. The basic concepts also apply to those valued individual contributors who have no direct reports and make up the professional backbone of many organizations.

And while we have been riveted on developing signature strengths, there are times when working on weaknesses is exactly the right thing to do. A chapter in the latter part of the book addresses this.

A frequently heard conclusion is that strengths can be taken too far, and when this happens, the strength actually flips over into becoming a weakness. Chances are we've all heard smart people say this. We present some data that address this interesting question. Once again, commonly held beliefs scatter and vanish in the face of data. There are some nuances regarding the definition of strengths, and we conclude that incorrect definitions of strengths have caused this myth to emerge.

Because strengths are not always accurately recognized by the person under consideration, the 360 instrument has become the tool of choice to help make better assessments of strengths and the individual's flat sides. We end the main portion of the book with our conclusions about 360-degree feedback instruments and how you can assess their value.

Appendixes

And then we round out the book with two appendixes.

In an earlier chapter, we examine the idea that strengths are set in concrete and there is not much hope of their being expanded or molded. In Appendix A, we explore this issue in much greater detail. We find the content fascinating because it addresses the question that never goes away: "Are leaders born or made?" Frankly, as a profession we've not generally done a good job of explaining the truth about this question. Here's a new effort at providing a more complete and accurate answer.

In Appendix B, we turn our attention to the history of the strengths movement. Not everyone loves history, but many of us do. And so in Appendix B, we provide a quick tour of the history of the strengths movement, which, we hope, will help to have greater clarity regarding the underpinnings of the strengths movement, and how our research fits into the broader picture.

What Leaders Can Learn from Their Strengths

As a leader who wants to become more effective, do I identify my weaknesses and chip away at them, or do I discover what I'm reasonably good at and strive to magnify those qualities? These first chapters answer those questions and provide evidence regarding the benefits of each approach.

Chapter 1 makes the case that organizations desperately need strong leaders because they make a measurable impact on virtually every quantifiable business outcome.

Chapter 2 provides data about the makeup of the highest-performing leaders and describes the role that profound strengths play in defining them. In this chapter, we explain the complex interplay between leadership strengths and weaknesses and the reasons for our emphasis on developing strengths. In parallel, however, we describe the benefits that are also gained by overcoming weaknesses.

Chapter 3 shows that strengths can be developed and examines the basic process by which that occurs. We introduce the concept that the methods that succeed in overcoming a weakness are quite different from those needed to develop a strength, including a cross-training approach to building on strengths that we describe as "nonlinear development."

Chapter 4 more fully explores the concept of cross-training, given that it is such a revolutionary approach to developing leadership skills.

Chapter 5 concludes this first part of the book by outlining the benefits from someone electing to work on strengths in contrast to the more traditional approach of working on weaknesses.

Organizations Flourish with Strong Leaders

The Measurable Impact of Being Exceptional

Have you ever been part of an organization where things were proceeding smoothly—where goals were achieved, people were productive, and the organization was doing reasonably well? Then a new leader came into the organization, and everything suddenly changed for the better. The energy level of employees went up substantially, pride in the organization increased, the effort and dedication of individuals jumped, bold objectives were enthusiastically accepted, and even greater results were achieved. The differences could be felt by everyone. Better yet, the accountants could measure the improvement.

Perhaps you also have had the opposite experience. You were in an organization where things were going reasonably well, and a new leader was introduced. You quickly saw things begin to fall apart. First you noticed high performers quitting; then conflicts became more apparent, work seemed much less important, and you were not having fun. Your colleagues skulked into corners, not wanting to be engaged. Overall satisfaction decreased. Grousing and carping criticism of the senior leaders became rampant. People receiving promotions were seemingly chosen because of politics, not performance. Management decisions felt arbitrary and unfair. Results began to slide, and your fellow employees became the cause of the problem as much as the economy or market conditions. Key employees were laid off, while the remaining people were asked to carry a bigger load. Results continued to decline, your job felt increasingly harder, and you began to think about escaping from this misery.

The Difference Can Be Measured

Those who have experienced great leadership or poor leadership have felt that difference. To a large extent, people know poor and great leadership when they personally experience it. Could these changes have been predicted? Are there clear correlations between the effectiveness of a leader and the success of an organization? Can great leadership be developed? If so, is there an efficient method to help leaders improve?

In extensive studies, we have demonstrated the clear connection between the effectiveness of a leader and a variety of important organizational outcomes. Bottom line, great leaders increase profit, drive up customer satisfaction, generate higher levels of engagement in their employees, reduce employee turnover, and develop stronger employees.

Big Questions About Extraordinary Leadership

As we turn our attention to what makes exceptional leaders, some important questions come into focus:

- Where exactly do exceptional leaders come from?

- Can such leaders actually be developed, or is this simply an issue of selecting a natural-born leader?

- How do organizations identify them?

- What do these leaders do differently from their colleagues?

- What can be done to develop more of those who make a huge, positive difference, while avoiding those that cause organizations to nosedive?

- Can we help existing leaders acquire the behaviors and traits of the best ones?

- Finally, why do some organizations succeed at producing a steady stream of such leaders, while others struggle with repeated missteps in selecting and developing them?

These are some of the questions we will attempt to address in this book.

Our Earlier Research

In our earlier book, *The Extraordinary Leader*, we examined the characteristics or competencies that most effectively separated the best leaders from the worst. To understand the key differences, we examined data from more than 20,000 leaders, who had been measured with a variety of 360-degree feedback instruments. Collectively these instruments included over 1,850 survey items describing various leadership behaviors. We had assessments from over 200,000 evaluators. Our analysis revealed 16 competencies that most effectively differentiated the best from the worst leaders as measured by their aggregate 360-degree feedback scores.

Further research led us to discover 49 survey items that accurately measure leaders' effectiveness at these specific competencies. These competencies described what bad leaders did that led to failure and what the best leaders did that guaranteed success. These assessments were completed by a leader's manager, peers, direct reports, and others, such as those two levels below the leader, former colleagues, customers, and suppliers.

Organizations Need Strong Leaders at All Levels

Since those discoveries, we have assessed the effectiveness of approximately 100,000 additional leaders in organizations of all sizes all over the world. In these assessments, we discovered some organizations with an abundance of great leaders. We have also experienced organizations where great leaders were so rare that it felt like they were headed for extinction. If great leaders were born with those qualities, then you might assume that organizations with an abundance of great leaders must have had a selection process that is extraordinary, while organizations with a dearth of great leaders must have a selection process so bad that it was incapable of selecting great leaders.

Selection Processes Seem Alike

Yet as we look at the selection processes of these different organizations, we cannot find any substantial difference in the processes or procedures between them. In fact, we know that leadership talent is much more likely to become apparent with years of experience in an organization, and inevitably those organizations with great leadership talent tend to promote from within and have employees with long tenure.

As you observe organizations with an abundance of great leadership talent, several differences become apparent.

1. Great leaders attract others with talent. Like magnets that are properly aligned, there is a huge attraction. Something clicks between them. Other competent leaders want to work with them.

2. Great leaders discover and pull out hidden abilities in those about them. Good qualities emerge. Strong teams develop, and collaboration abounds.

3. Great leaders tend to stay and build. Not only are they initially attracted to the organization and the other leaders in it, but they thrive in place, build off each other, and grow the garden they're in. They aren't looking to quickly hop to another challenge. Their continued presence brings stability, confidence, and steadiness to the organization.

Poor leaders are the polar opposites. Their impact is leaden. Like every other weight, their effect is to hold things down. People become immobile. And like the lead shield used by an x-ray technician to cover the patient, these leaders block energy from passing through.

As you observe organizations with a dearth of leadership talent, other differences emerge:

1. The leaders aren't able to attract the best talent. Just as opposite polarities result in magnetic attraction, identical polarities cause magnetic repulsion. Great leaders sense early in the selection process that these toxic organizations will not make a great landing spot. In fact, unconfident leaders in these organizations are highly unlikely to recruit potentially more effective leaders than themselves.

2. The leaders aren't able to draw out the best in those around them. It isn't unusual for those around the leader to feel stifled and constrained by the boss. Unaligned, counterproductive individual and team efforts are often abundant and highly visible, and the resulting frustrations become openly discussed.

3. There is regular turnover in leadership. When good leaders occasionally blossom, they tend to move on. More often, their leadership shortcomings result in poor organizational performance. This leads to rotational leadership, as attempts are made to turn around the results. Stability, confidence, and steadiness are absent, further inhibiting organizational performance.

Organizations Are Layered

In general, leadership effectiveness increases as you move to higher levels in organizations. While there are exceptions to this rule, the trend is remarkably consistent and clear. Leaders at the top of an organization tend to be rated more highly by the collective colleagues than their direct reports. These direct reports in turn tend to be rated more highly than those who report to them, and that pattern cascades through the organization.

In a study of 5,285 leaders working in five different organizations, we examined the effectiveness of leaders at different levels of these organizations. This measure of leadership effectiveness was derived from our research on extraordinary leaders, utilizing 360-degree feedback instruments. Results from each organization were examined, and the graph in Figure 1.1 shows the average difference by level.

High and Low Ceilings

The average gap between levels of management is 14.5 percentile points. Using that as an average metric, if an organization wanted leaders at the fourth level of management to be at the 50th percentile (just average), the top level of leaders would need to be at the 94th percentile in terms of their average leadership effectiveness.

Figure 1.1 Leadership Effectiveness by Level

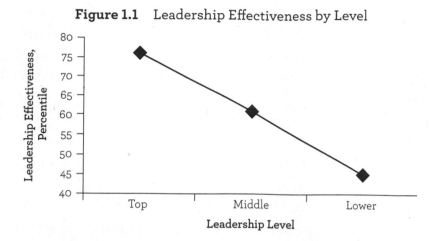

We have worked with organizations in which the senior team had overall effectiveness scores hovering at the 65th percentile. That means that in all likelihood the next lower level will be at the 50th percentile, and each successive layer well below that. Indeed, that is what occurred. The consequences were far reaching. Employee commitment scores in those organizations were at the 32nd percentile.

Reducing the Gap

Not every organization had large gaps between levels. A handful of organizations only had gaps of 3 to 5 percentile points between levels. This small gap created a dramatic shift upward in the effectiveness of leaders at all levels. It became apparent that the smaller gap was the result of several differences in these organizations.

First was selecting the right people as leaders. Some organizations select leaders based only on financial indicators. But the superior organizations had talent management processes that looked beyond the numbers. They also cared about how people achieved those numbers.

Second, these talent management processes identified a clear set of desirable leadership competencies. Having this well-defined set of competencies created a common behavioral target and language that enabled these organizations to better define leadership effectiveness.

Third, senior executives believed that a significant part of all leaders' jobs was the development of their direct reports. They felt it was a line-management responsibility and not the responsibility of human resources. Human resources, they felt, provides support to make this happen, but that both the responsibility and accountability were clearly with the line managers. Because of this belief, feedback was frequent, and development was welcomed and encouraged.

Fourth, the bar for effective leadership was set high. The expectation was that the leaders needed to be outstanding, and not merely adequate or good, and that everyone, regardless of position or level in the organization, could improve.

Measuring the Impact of Leadership

What is the effect of exceptional leadership on organizational performance? In this section, we present studies showing the impact of leadership on bottom-line results.

Sales

The lifeblood of commercial organizations is sales. Sales leaders are viewed as a critical factor in the success of every sales organization. A study, summarized in Figure 1.2, shows the relationship between a sales leader's leadership effectiveness and the total sales for the sales leader's unit within the organization. More than most other functions or outcomes in organizations, sales can be accurately and easily measured. While there are always some gray areas, the data are generally available and objective.

In Figure 1.2, the overall leadership effectiveness, shown on the horizontal axis, is based on the overall 360-degree feedback scores ob-

Figure 1.2 Impact of Leadership Effectiveness on Team Sales

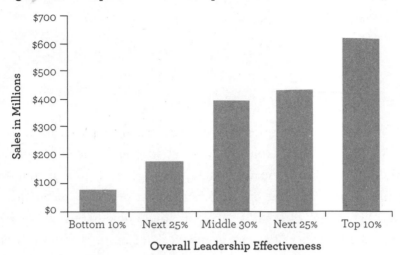

tained by these leaders. These scores were separated to represent five levels of effectiveness, as perceived by those rating the leaders. These were then plotted against actual dollar revenue results on the vertical axis.

This is an instructive study showing that the teams being led by the best sales leaders generate six times the sales of the teams being led by the worst leaders. It is easy to quantify the direct and significant impact of leadership on a unit's business results when viewing the outcomes of this study.

Employee Engagement, Satisfaction, and Commitment

As all organizations look for the magic bullet to improve the engagement, satisfaction, and commitment levels of employees, various approaches are attempted. These include:

- Elevated pay
- Richer benefits
- Additional training and development opportunities

- Enhanced working conditions
- State-of-the-art equipment
- Flexible schedules
- Childcare
- Additional focus on work-life balance

All of the above appear to have some, though modest, impact.

In all our research to predict the satisfied, engaged, and committed employee versus the dissatisfied, disengaged, and uncommitted employee, one variable emerged as the best predictor of the differences. That one variable is "Who is your immediate supervisor?" Knowing the leader of a work group explains more variability in satisfaction, engagement, and commitment than any other elements we have analyzed.

In a study of 2,865 leaders within a large financial services company, the leadership effectiveness of each leader was evaluated by his or her direct reports. Those same direct reports were asked to rate their own levels of satisfaction, engagement, and commitment. Because the study focused specifically on the results from one organization, the consistency of the data demonstrates the relationship between leadership and employee satisfaction, engagement, and commitment.

As shown in Figure 1.3, the worst leaders (those at the 10th percentile or lower) had employees with a satisfaction, engagement, and commitment level at the 4th percentile. These were the employees who were mumbling about hating their jobs, who were frustrated at work, who were generally unmotivated, and who often let everyone around them know it. The best leaders had the complete opposite situation, with their employees scoring at the 92nd percentile.

While many factors impact employee satisfaction, engagement, and commitment, the one factor that every organization ought to put first is the effectiveness of leaders. Having excellent rewards, career paths, and a pleasant work environment will make very little differ-

Figure 1.3 The Relationship Between Leadership and Employee Satisfaction, Engagement, and Commitment

ence to employees with a poor leader. The effectiveness of the leader sets the stage to allow other factors to be valued.

We have conducted this study hundreds of times in different geographies and organizations and found the same results—regardless of whether the study was done in the United States, United Kingdom, Netherlands, Spain, United Arab Emirates, or India. Similarly, it made no difference whether the industry was financial services, manufacturing, high technology, government, university, hospitals, foods, or oil; again the results were the same. Finally, it made no difference if the organization employed 225,000 or 250 people; the same trends existed.

Highly Committed Team Members

As a variation of the above study, we decided to study those employees who described themselves as being highly committed. On a question that asked them to describe their level of commitment to the organization, the employees in this group rated themselves "five" on a five-point scale.

Past analysis has shown that these are the employees who come to work early and stay late. They are excited by challenging assignments. They are enthusiastic and willing to do more, and typically they have a very positive attitude overall. Frankly, we were surprised to find that even the worst leaders had 13 percent of their employees who fell into this category. A logical question would be, "How did they get any?"

Our hypothesis is that either certain people are born highly committed, or they learn this at an early age from their parents or from their environment. Regardless of the circumstance in which they are placed, the employees in this group continue to be highly committed. We concluded that if an organization just randomly hired people from the general workforce population, it would find that about 13 percent of that group would be "highly committed," regardless of their leader's effectiveness.

As you can see from Figure 1.4, average leaders, those around the 50th percentile, have approximately 30 percent of their employees who are highly committed, whereas the best have more than 60 percent of their teams who are highly committed. If you ask leaders about the impact of moving from 13 percent to 30 percent of highly committed employees—

Figure 1.4 The Relationship Between Leadership and Highly Committed Team Members

and then upward to 60 percent of highly committed employees—their answers are consistent. Without hesitation, they confirm that their ability to get projects done on time and on budget increases. Productivity shoots up. Concurrently, innovation and initiative skyrocket.

Leadership and the Bottom Line

An abundance of research confirms the relationship between the satisfaction and engagement of employees and the level of satisfaction of customers. Rucci, Kim, and Quinn found what they called "the employee-customer-profit chain" at Sears.[1] Their study found that employee behaviors affected customer behaviors, which in turn affected company financial performance. Specifically, when employee satisfaction measures improved by 5 percent, then customer satisfaction improved by 1.3 percent, which led to a 0.5 percent improvement in store revenue. Some might see that number and wonder if that is a truly significant improvement, but when you consider that this was a chain of retail stores that at the time had $50 billion per year in revenue, every 5 percent improvement in employee satisfaction could amount to $250 million in added revenue.

The chain of employee satisfaction that leads to customer satisfaction is understandable in a retail environment. We've all undoubtedly experienced both dissatisfaction and satisfaction in these situations, and our experience is largely dependent on the interactions we have with the retail employees.

The dissatisfaction scenario is probably familiar:

- We first have difficulty even finding someone to help.
- When we do, the person makes us feel like we're interrupting more important tasks he or she is doing.
- And when we are ready to make a purchase, the person grudgingly puts aside whatever he or she is doing in order to take our money.

On the other hand, chances are you have also been the beneficiary of great retail service:

- Pleasant and welcoming offers to provide assistance
- A focus on meeting our needs that makes us feel like the person is there to help only us
- A smooth, courteous, and attentive checkout process

There's no question that our buying patterns and potential repeat purchases are affected by the customer experience delivered by the retail employee.

When customers enter a store where employees are frustrated and unmotivated, it affects their buying habits and their willingness to return and purchase more items. Pleasant, considerate, helpful, and knowledgeable sales associates have a positive effect on customers. The behaviors of these sales associates encourage customers to buy more and to come back. Figure 1.5 sums up the results of the study, showing the effect of employee satisfaction on customer satisfaction and ultimately store profits.

This study has been replicated by other retailers such as JCPenney and Best Buy. Likewise, similar studies have been conducted by Marriott in the hospitality industry with similar outcomes.

Figure 1.5 Employee Satisfaction Impacts Customer Satisfaction, Which, in Turn, Affects Store Profits

Employee Engagement and Commitment and Customer

What about the impact of customer satisfaction in other, nonretail organizations? A large telecommunication company collected a variety of customer satisfaction ratings. In this industry, customer satisfaction impacts customer retention, which is a major driving force in profitability. The question the company wanted to answer was what factors impacted the satisfaction of customers?

For this study, we selected a group of 81 leaders who had received 360-degree feedback from their immediate managers, peers, direct reports, and others. In this analysis, the level of employee engagement and commitment of the direct reports for each of the 81 managers was assessed. The graph in Figure 1.6 displays the results.

Just as there was in the much larger study reported earlier, for this smaller group of 81 managers, there was a clear relationship between a leader's effectiveness and the level of engagement and commitment of their direct reports. In this case, the direct reports of the worst leaders had engagement and commitment levels at the 29th percentile, while

Figure 1.6   Employee Engagement and Commitment

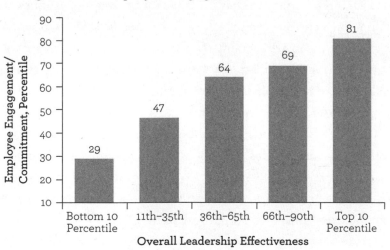

the best leaders were at the 81st percentile. Although each manager received customer satisfaction ratings, the managers realized that it was their direct reports who had the greatest involvement with customers. A more detailed analysis of this next level down, the direct reports, revealed useful information in regard to the intention of those direct reports to leave the organization.

Intention to Leave the Organization

In this follow-on study with the subordinates of the same 81 managers, we tabulated the percentage of the members of this subordinate group who were considering quitting their jobs and moving to another organization. (When the job market is healthy, this measurement of intention to leave is an excellent predictor of turnover. When jobs are available, about 50 percent of the people who think about quitting actually quit within 18 months.)

This second study showed a significant relationship between a leader's effectiveness and the percentage of direct reports who were thinking about leaving the organization (see Figure 1.7). Losing talented sales representatives has a significant impact on customer satisfaction. Each customer in the study had a specific sales representative assigned to his or her account. Turnover required a customer to develop a relationship with a new sales representative. The relationship would have to be rebuilt as the new representative tried to understand the specific needs of the customer.

Possibly just as damaging as the actual loss of talented employees, another consequence this study points to is the impact on employees whose frustration causes them to consider quitting. While these employees have not left the company, their passion and their willingness to go the extra mile have probably departed. Thinking about quitting can create a negative attitude shift, causing employee performance to

Figure 1.7   Intention to Leave

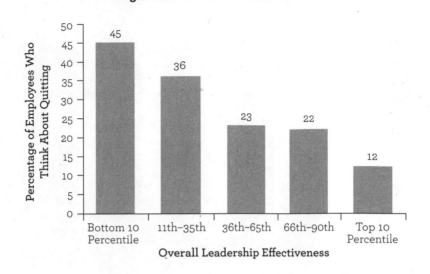

decline. Note from the graph in Figure 1.7 that 45 percent of the employees who worked for the worst leaders were thinking about quitting, compared with only 12 percent, or approximately one-fourth as many, of employees who worked for the best leaders.

Customer Satisfaction Ratings

The final study examined the customer satisfaction rating versus the overall leadership effectiveness scores. Because of the linkages between leadership effectiveness, employee satisfaction, and customer satisfaction, it should not be surprising that these ratings followed the same trend, with the worst leaders receiving significantly lower customer satisfaction ratings and the best receiving substantially higher ratings (see Figure 1.8).

This research on the correlation of overall leadership effectiveness, as measured by a 360-degree survey, with several other operational dimensions, reinforces the conclusions from previous research that

Figure 1.8   Customer Satisfaction Ratings

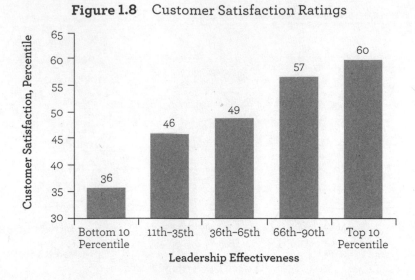

leadership affects employee commitment, satisfaction, and intention to stay in the organization, which affects customer satisfaction.

This relationship is shown graphically in Figure 1.9. The research also strongly suggests that this linkage is applicable to many other industries, not just the retail and hospitality sectors.

Figure 1.9   Leadership Effectiveness Impacts
Employee Satisfaction and Retention, Which,
in Turn, Impacts Customer Satisfaction

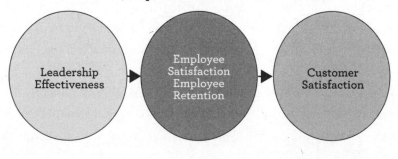

Conclusion

Our belief is that the success of an organization is inseparably tied to the skills and abilities of its leaders. There is compelling evidence to show the correlation between leadership effectiveness and essential organizational outcomes. We find it amusing that leadership is often referred to as a "soft skill." Accounting, technical knowledge, and engineering abilities are considered hard skills, but leadership a soft one. Often, the assumption with this description is that there is a very direct connection between these hard skills and organizational performance. Poor engineering creates bad products; poor accounting and financial decisions can negatively impact the market value of an organization. We take the position that there is an equally clear and measurable impact of leadership effectiveness on bottom-line results.

CHAPTER 2

Why Emphasize Strengths?

The Complex Interplay Between Strengths and High-Performing Leaders

Most people have had the experience of receiving performance evaluations from their bosses. As we ask people to reflect on that experience, the process for most seems similar. It goes something like this:

> The boss schedules the meeting with an announcement that says, "It's time for our annual performance discussion."
>
> The boss begins the discussion by talking about this person's accomplishments and positive qualities. As the boss reviews the positive elements of past performance, the person thinks, "You're so right; I am really good at that. I'm happy that you've noticed what I do well." The person begins to think, "I like this performance discussion."

Then the boss says, "But," and the conversation heads in a somewhat different direction. The boss begins listing some of the person's performance shortfalls and weaknesses. The conversation becomes less pleasant. At the end of the review, the person leaves the office with a very clear message in mind: "If you want a better performance rating, a fatter raise, or a promotion sometime in the future, you need to fix your weaknesses!"

As we work with people in organizations across the world and describe that experience, virtually everyone can identify with it. People's remarks are invariably something to the effect of: "That's exactly the way things are done here." Further, it would appear that some combination of family upbringing, schooling, and experience working in various organizations has reinforced and confirmed the message that "improvement means fixing weaknesses."

The Universal Pattern of Focusing on Weaknesses

For the past several decades, we have worked in firms that were focused in large measure on helping managers and key professional associates identify their weaknesses and then fix them. (When we weren't doing that, we were teaching new managers the basic fundamentals of how to survive in their new roles.) We developed assessments that identified strengths or weaknesses with equal effectiveness. But the fact of the matter was that they were used primarily to identify weaknesses. That's what people wanted to know. The unspoken assumption was that whatever strengths people possessed were just there, whether through personal effort or some divine injection, and would take care of themselves. What was of far greater concern was to hunt down and eradicate weaknesses.

For those participants new to leadership roles, we also developed training that showed examples of good behavior and bad behavior and encouraged participants to adopt the good behaviors and avoid and correct the bad behaviors. Our focus was to get leaders to a solid ground where they would avoid getting into trouble. In hindsight, it was not to have them perform like the exceptional leaders in the top 10 percent of leaders in the organization, but much more to avoid behaving like the bottom 10 percent.

Much of our traditional educational experience is based on this same model (though there are selected areas in which the objective is to strive for excellence). Many parenting practices follow this same approach, and it seems universal across the world. We're thinking of the oft-recurring event of a child bringing home a report card. If we take the example of the report card with many As and Bs and one lone C, what is the likely topic of conversation in most households? Is it a celebration of the As? Or is it about the Bs and how you could move some of them to an A? Or is it more focused on the lone C? We've asked individuals from countries and cultures all over the world about their childhood "report card" experiences and, from all the responses we get (usually accompanied with a big smile), parents being riveted on the C seems to be a universal situational response.

Working on Weaknesses Can Sometimes Be the Right Approach

One of the reasons that may explain why a weakness-focused approach is so prevalent is that sometimes it is the right approach. We will explore this more fully in a later chapter. But here's the bottom line: if a leader has some trait or competency that is a profound weakness, and this behavior is both important on the job and readily observed by others, this could be considered a fatal flaw. One or more fatal flaws have the potential to sink this person's career unless those flaws are fixed.

Kevin is a salesperson who is very good in one-on-one discussions and in building individual relationships. However, his company recently reorganized the sales team and selling process, requiring him to now make regular presentations to large groups. Unfortunately, he has lots of trouble communicating effectively to groups of almost any size. Because he gets very nervous when he has to be "on stage," he regularly loses his train of thought as he is presenting, and he has difficulty responding to any questions. Since group presentations are now a critical part of his job and his lack of skill at making them is easily observed, this change has uncovered a profound weakness and a potential fatal flaw for Kevin. If he can't quickly develop a competency in this area, at best he'll have trouble hitting his sales targets; at worst he may lose his job.

Jane, who works in a different department but at the same company as Kevin, has similar difficulties when asked to present to groups. However, as a software developer, the nature of her job is such that she is rarely asked to make group presentations. Unlike for Kevin, it's not even important in Jane's job that she be particularly skilled at making them. She's also found that when it is necessary, the presentations are usually done in a group with her colleagues, and they are easily able to support her. Although Jane's group presentation skills may be considered a profound weakness because they are of such little importance and used so rarely in her position, that weakness is not likely to be considered a fatal flaw.

Adversaries, on discovering a huge chink in someone's armor, are prone to take advantage of it. In baseball, for example, a batter may be an otherwise outstanding hitter, unless the opposing pitcher throws a sinker high over the plate. If the batter doesn't remedy that deficiency, he is prone to get that pitch tossed at him with ever-greater frequency by more and more opposing pitchers. The batter is virtually guaranteed a steady stream of sinkers in that very location. Fixing that fatal flaw will be critical to the batter's success.

When to Work on Weaknesses

If leaders have significant weaknesses, ones that could be considered fatal flaws, improving those weaknesses can have a substantial positive impact on their overall effectiveness. Fixing them can keep them from being negatively singled out. For a new manager, correcting the weakness helps to avoid making further serious mistakes related to the flaw. Fixing it gets the manager up to ground zero. But this constitutes the largest problem with a weakness focus. Its misplaced use and overuse can turn it into a trap that might be described as an "attractive hazard." Although it gets you to a position where this behavior is no longer detracting from your overall performance, it doesn't elevate you much beyond that. That's where working on strengths comes into play. (Later chapters in this book address when and how to work on correcting weaknesses.)

Strengths Make Extraordinary Leaders

The first notable departure from this practice of working on weaknesses and deficiencies was found in the book *In Search of Excellence* by Tom Peters and Robert Waterman, Jr. It proposed a new tack of looking at those practices that seemed to drive some organizations to be leaders in their industry. While their research was later acknowledged to have been fudged a bit, their concepts made a huge impact on management thinking in the 1980s. It began an entirely new philosophy of seeking excellence.

Several years ago, we began to look at extraordinary leaders, and we published our findings in our book, *The Extraordinary Leader*. These were leaders who were rated by their managers, peers, direct reports, and others as being in the top 10 percent of all the leaders they knew. As we analyzed the data, we came to a startling but, we thought, logical conclusion. What made a leader great was the presence of strengths, not the absence of weaknesses. Great leaders did a few things exceptionally well.

Exceptional Leaders Are Not Perfect

There is one thing that no longer surprises us when we share these data with others. As we get people to identify the best leaders they have known or with whom they've worked, we ask them if these great leaders had any weaknesses. The answer is always the same, "Yes—they were not perfect." Our next question is, "If they had weaknesses, what made them so exceptional?" The answer is always that it was their strengths. It was what they did extremely well that made the difference and always far outweighed any weaknesses they may have had. What began to be clear to us then and what has become clearer to us now is that if people spend all their time focusing on fixing weaknesses, their potential strengths will never become profound strengths. It is that shift in focus—from trying not to be below average on anything to, instead, being outstanding at relatively few behaviors—that makes such a huge impact on others and causes these leaders to be viewed as exceptional.

READER'S EXERCISE

We invite you to stop reading for a few moments and do the following:

Think about the best leader you ever worked for. Take a moment and identify the competency areas in which that leader was extraordinarily good. How many strengths can you identify?

Strengths: _____

_____

_____

_____

_____

_____

How many weaknesses can you identify?

Weaknesses: _____

_____

_____

_____

_____

_____

If you are like most people with whom we have conducted similar exercises, you will readily see that this leader whom you admire also had some qualities that were not exactly perfect. It appears that these deficiencies were not fatal flaws, and these imperfections were swamped by a number of profound strengths that this person possessed.

We see many empirical examples of this in the workplace. The late Steve Jobs seems to be a poster child for this principle. By all reports, he possessed some behaviors that were not ideal for a CEO to have. He was sometimes rude, abrasive, unreasonable, and tyrannical. But he was an incredible visionary who possessed a passion for extremely user-friendly products. He devoted great attention to the details of these products and set very high standards for the organization regarding the quality and design of every product. In short, his strengths trumped his weaknesses. Had he been devoid of weaknesses, but not possessing such strengths, he likely would not have had as much impact as he did.

The Only Pathway to Exceptional Leadership

A fundamental premise of this book is that the best-in-class leaders are those who possess and regularly utilize five or more powerful strengths that matter. There are those who believe that there are other ways to get there. We do not believe there are other paths. We can't find a single example of someone perceived as an exceptional leader who wasn't profoundly good in several areas important in the job.

What Doesn't Work

By way of example, here are two approaches that may seem logical at first blush, but simply do not work:

Eliminating Any Serious Weaknesses or Fatal Flaws

This is the person who has fixed some fatal flaws and no longer has scores on a 360 that range from the 1st to the 10th percentile. Fixing a fatal flaw is an important effort since you just can't be awful at some leadership competency important to your job and still succeed in being a highly effective leader. But simply erasing one or two egregious weaknesses, by itself, does not turn you into an extraordinary leader.

We all know horror stories about bad bosses. These range from the boss who screams, shouts, berates, and throws things across the room, to bosses who will never make a decision, to bosses who fail to take responsibility for their actions. A currently popular TV show, *The Office*, painfully spoofs a bad boss who totally lacks self-awareness and constantly engages in inappropriate interactions with his subordinates.

But let's assume for a moment that we could eradicate these really bad behaviors. Would that create an inspiring, highly effective leader? The answer is obviously no. Simply removing inappropriate behavior brings you to ground zero. It eliminates behaviors that detract, but that does not immediately create a leader who makes you feel truly inspired. It is true that eliminating a weakness may enable an individual's strengths to finally come shining through, and that helps; but there is more to being an exceptional leader than the absence of weaknesses.

For example, imagine that it was determined that five competencies, A, B, C, D, and E, were critical to a particular leader's performance and effectiveness on the job. If the absence of weaknesses was the route to exceptional leadership, you could logically conclude that leaders would be highly effective if they were average at (i.e., no weaknesses in) each of the five competencies. That's obviously not correct. Yet we find that many leaders and their organizations continue to target their development efforts at attaining "average" and on eliminating weaknesses.

Being Good at Virtually All Leadership Competencies

Let's assume a leader has no score on a 360 that is below the 40th percentile, but also has nothing above the 70th percentile. This is clearly better than not being good at a wide variety of leadership competencies. A leader like this might be called a jack-of-all-trades, good at virtually everything, "but a master of none." But this works only slightly better than being devoid of weakness.

In most large organizations that have existed for a decade or more, there is some congenial, well-liked manager who is often known as "good old _____." (You can fill in the name.) This manager doesn't initiate new projects. This manager's group is performing adequately, but not brilliantly. Nothing stands out about this individual positively or negatively, nor does anything stand out regarding the performance of the group he or she leads.

We repeat, excellent leadership is all about someone possessing, at a minimum, a small number of profound strengths that elevate that person above the others. This is the only set of conditions we have found that creates an exceptional leader.

Strengths Defined

Countless adjectives and phrases exist to describe various dimensions of a leader's behavior. How about *bravery, caution, courage, curiosity, loyalty, initiative, enthusiasm, work ethic, generosity, caring, innovativeness, integrity, sound judgment*—you get the message—and the list goes on. But what is it that constitutes the strengths that actually define a powerful leader?

Various scholars have contemplated this issue and have proposed several elements that define a strength.[1] These are:

1. A trait that is performed well, similar to the way it is performed by the top 10 or 20 percent of leaders in a given population.

2. A trait that is successfully used in diverse situations or settings.

3. A trait that endures over time.

4. A trait that produces positive outcomes consistently. The results are not erratic.

5. A trait that the individual enjoys using.

6. A trait that is widely valued for its intrinsic worth, not only for its outcomes.

7. A trait that transcends a specific culture.

8. A trait that does not compete with or diminish other traits.

9. A trait that is generally developed by focused effort and deliberate practice.

Strengths Versus Talents

The importance of this definition of *strengths* is that it goes well beyond qualities that have often been defined as talents. We define *talents* as qualities that are hardwired in people. For example, a quick reaction time is in large measure genetically determined. If you blow a puff of air into an infant's face and measure the time the infant takes to blink, there are variations in that reaction time, and these persist through life. Some athletic activities require this talent. Some children are born with perfect pitch. A smaller number of children are born with absolute pitch, the ability to hear a sound and name the note on a piano; or conversely to be asked to sing a "G" and to be able to sing that note correctly. Attempts to teach this skill to people beyond the age of eight have consistently failed. Intelligence is inborn to some degree. IQ can be improved through hard work, but there appear to be general ranges or boundaries in which that improvement occurs. Characteristics like these appear not to be learned, but to be genetically determined.

These talents do not lend themselves to development. (We recognize that the word *talent* is extremely confusing, because it is often used in our popular culture to describe abilities that can be developed, such as musical talent or athletic talent. Both of these have major components that clearly can be developed via extensive practice.)

Empirically Identified Leadership Strengths

Our research on leadership competencies sought to discover those behaviors and traits that truly differentiated high performers from those who were not. In Chapter 6 we introduce and describe in more detail these "16 differentiating competencies" that most distinguish the exceptional leaders. These competencies meet the criteria described in the previous section and, while we will not address here each of the criteria for each competency, a few of the criteria deserve special attention:

- The leadership competencies that we'll describe are valid in every culture we've studied. Both our statistical research and our work providing leadership coaching to individual managers and executives confirm this conclusion.

  These studies and coaching efforts have included leaders not only from North America, but from Latin America, the Middle East, Asia, Africa, Australia, and Europe.

- These differentiating competencies are valued in their own right. Thus high integrity seems valued (if not always practiced) in nearly every culture. The same holds for those who are driven to produce good results, those who are technically competent, those who can solve problems, those who are innovative, and those who communicate effectively.

- These behaviors consistently produce positive outcomes. They are not sporadic or situational. When used well, each one of these behaviors has a positive result. For example, innovation always has a positive payout. So does effective problem solving, as does the willingness to display initiative.

- Each of the differentiating competencies that we have identified does not appear to detract from other strengths. Being an excellent strategic thinker does not make someone less effective in inspiring and motivating to high performance. Nor does the perception of having great technical expertise detract from being perceived as having high character and integrity.

- The existence of the differentiating competency in one leader doesn't diminish or restrict its appearance in another. Having a CEO who is perceived as an inspirational leader doesn't prevent her direct reports from also being seen as inspirational. In fact, as discussed in other chapters, the existence of profound strengths in a leader often attracts others with similar strengths. Widespread occurrence of a particular strength or set of strengths, especially when valued and recognized by an organization, may become a cultural strength and differentiator. 3M and Apple, for example, appear to have that with innovation. General Electric and Southwest Airlines are generally perceived as organizations that excel in driving for results.

- The differentiating competencies that we have identified are not hardwired in individuals at birth. There is no evidence that they are genetically determined. They do not dramatically appear at an early age. Instead they evolve, and concerted effort such as extensive practice leads to improvement.

For our purposes then, we will define leadership strengths as those qualities that are highly valued in most cultures, that are valued in their own right, that can be developed through focused effort, that may be found in multiple leaders of an organization, and that have been shown to separate those perceived as the highest-performing leaders from those perceived as average or poor leaders.

Martin Seligman noted, "I believe that the highest success in living and the deepest emotional satisfaction comes from building and using your signature strengths." That principle applies to leaders. Those leaders with whom we interact who are the most energized and productive fit this description exactly. They have deliberately built these strengths, and they are in a place to use their signature strengths.

The Interplay of Strengths and Weaknesses

There is clearly an important interaction between strengths and weaknesses. We doubt that any reader will be surprised if we state that—everything else being equal—a leader who possesses multiple weaknesses will perform at a lower level than someone who does not display such faults. Conversely, the leader who possesses several strengths will perform at a much higher level than those lacking such strengths.

The graphs in Figures 2.1 to 2.3 illustrate that point. Figure 2.1 compares the impact of profound weaknesses and strengths on the level of employee satisfaction, engagement, and commitment as measured from our global database. This study was done with some 19,905 managers worldwide and plots the results of 360-degree feedback data against an independent measure of employee satisfaction, engagement, and commitment.

Our 360-degree feedback instrument includes a section that measures employee commitment. These questions are given only to the direct reports (subordinates) of the participating manager. The questions ask how the individual employees feel about the organization. The questions ask about whether those employees would recommend the organization to a friend, whether they believe the organization will achieve its strategic goals, and whether, all in all, they believe their organization is a good place to work. Because these questions are focused on the organization, rather than the manager, they are quite different from the remaining items in the questionnaire. The impact of weaknesses and strengths becomes readily apparent when compared

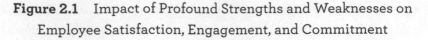

Figure 2.1 Impact of Profound Strengths and Weaknesses on Employee Satisfaction, Engagement, and Commitment

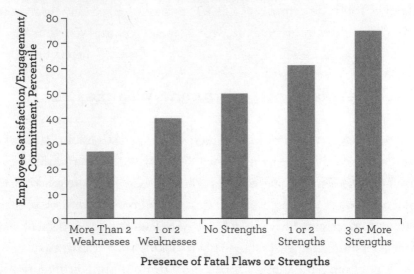

Note: Profound weaknesses are competencies rated at or below the 10th percentile. Profound strengths are competencies rated at or above the 90th percentile.

with the overall level of commitment and satisfaction of a leader's direct reports.

Currently, an enormous amount of attention in organizations around the world is being paid to employee engagement and commitment. Both have been shown to have a profound effect on the performance of an organization and obviously relate to the level of productivity and performance. As we noted in Chapter 1, in study after study, the level of employee engagement has been shown to drive overall customer satisfaction, which in turn increases revenue and ultimate profitability.

Performance Appraisal Ratings

Figure 2.2 conveys a similar message regarding the interplay between profound weaknesses and strengths when managers were rated as "far exceeding their goals" by their bosses in their performance appraisal process. This study, done at a large telecommunications company, accessed data from 2,179 leaders where there were both 360 results and promotional performance ratings for all leaders. There were four different ratings that managers could be given, but only 14 percent received the highest performance rating. Of all those managers having more than two weaknesses, just 8 percent were rated as "far exceeding their goals" by their managers. In the group of managers having three or more strengths, on the other hand, we found that more than 30 percent of them were rated as "far exceeding their goals" by their managers.

A final piece of important data is the significant correlation we found between the overall effectiveness of leaders and the number of strengths they possess. In this study, we examined data from 24,657 leaders from a global database. We looked at the impact of an increasing number of profound strengths on an overall assessment of a leader's ability. Figure 2.3 describes this relationship.

It is clear that going beyond five strengths ceases to make much of a difference. The good news is that a relatively small number of pro-

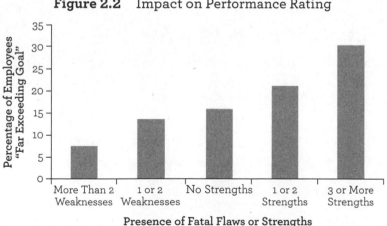

Figure 2.2 Impact on Performance Rating

Note: Profound weaknesses are competencies rated at or below the 10th percentile. Profound strengths are competencies rated at or above the 90th percentile.

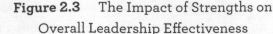

Figure 2.3   The Impact of Strengths on
Overall Leadership Effectiveness

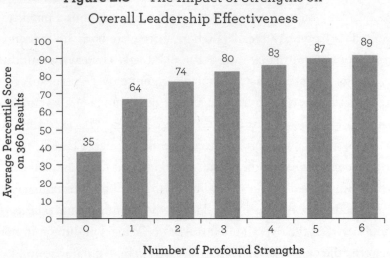

Note: Profound strengths are competencies rated at or above the 90th percentile.

found strengths are all that is required for a leader to be viewed in the top 10 percent of leaders in any organization.

What was clear in all three studies described above was the impact of having a profound strength or profound weakness. In our studies, it did not appear to matter which of the 16 differentiating competencies was such a strength or weakness. Utilizing any valued behavior extremely well or poorly made a huge difference.

Why We Emphasize Strengths

Our decision to emphasize the development of strengths is based on several factors. First, the above data show that regardless of how much effort people spend on correcting weaknesses, it will only bring them to a certain midpoint on the overall measure of effectiveness.

A second reason to focus on strengths is illustrated by an experience one of the authors had with a group of bankers. This meeting of more than 65 key people was held in a relaxed setting on the shores of Lake Tahoe. The members of the group were asked to write down a capability that, if executed with a high level of skill and proficiency, would have a great impact on their ability to be successful in their current job. In other words, they were asked, "What do you need to do well to be successful?" Each participant pondered this question for a few minutes. Fortunately all were able to quickly select a capability and write it down.

In the prior month, all the participants had completed their performance reviews with their managers. The next question posed to the group was, "How many of you in your most recent performance review with your manager talked about that one capability that would help you to be more successful?" Only five hands in the group of 65 raised up. What did the other 60 people in the group discuss? The conversation may have been about other competencies. Or it is possible that the focus of their conversation was on a weakness. The point is that whatever was discussed was not seen as a key to their being successful. Our preoccupation with fixing weaknesses causes managers to focus on asking people to improve capabilities based solely on the fact that they are weaknesses, rather than their importance to the success of an individual. Oftentimes capabilities that will make a person eminently successful are things we already do fairly well, but when these capabilities are improved, they would lead to dramatically more success.

The Distribution of Strengths and Weaknesses Among Leaders

While this book focuses primarily on the importance of strengths and how to better develop them, we don't want to be Pollyannas and pretend that weaknesses are not important. Chapter 12 delves into this more deeply. But it cannot be said too often—if you are aware of someone (including yourself) who possesses a fatal flaw, and you want to help the person to be more effective, begin with that.

Nor do we want to communicate the idea that having profound weaknesses is a rare exception in leadership groups. To the contrary, about the same number of people have profound weaknesses (a competency in the lowest 10 percent for all who have been assessed with the instrument) as those who possess profound strengths (a competency in the highest 10 percent). Figure 2.4, based on data from over 24,000 global leaders, shows how the population of leaders is basically a pie cut in three pieces. A thinner slice, one with 28 percent of the pie, represents those possessing one or more profound weakness. The second piece of the pie, which has 35 percent of the leaders, represents those who possess one or more profound strengths. The biggest slice of the pie is the group in the middle, which has 37 percent of the population. This group possesses neither profound strengths nor profound weaknesses.

We believe that those who do not possess a fatal flaw should focus their attention on developing strengths. At the very most, only 28 percent of a group of leaders should be focused on addressing a profound weaknesses, probably a good deal less. Why? Simply possessing a score in the bottom 10 percent of all leaders may not describe a

Figure 2.4 Percentage of Leaders with Profound Strengths and Weaknesses

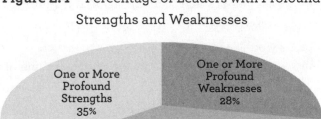

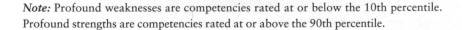

Note: Profound weaknesses are competencies rated at or below the 10th percentile. Profound strengths are competencies rated at or above the 90th percentile.

leader with a fatal flaw. The low score may be in some area that is not terribly important to the individual's job.

What differentiates a weakness from a fatal flaw? To answer this, let's take as an example an operations director who is not perceived by others as highly effective on strategic thinking. But this lack of skill in strategic thinking may have little consequence to this person's job success. Would we call it a weakness? Yes. A fatal flaw? No. An accounting manager whose team is primarily responsible for efficiently producing standard reports for internal use may not be a very powerful communicator. Her having a low score on this competency would likely not have a serious impact on how her performance is viewed in her current role and would probably not be considered a fatal flaw. However, this very same skill may be absolutely critical for her boss, the company's CFO, to possess. Not having it would likely be a fatal flaw. Why the difference? The CFO makes regular presentations to the board of directors and speaks weekly to external investors about the performance of the company.

The Role of Strengths in Understanding Leadership

An academic interest in the study of leadership is something of fairly recent origin. Schools of business have long included departments of management, but only relatively recently have they focused on leadership.

Many of the bedrock principles of business management had many similarities to the historic practice of medicine. Management, like medicine, was largely about finding exceptions and focusing attention on things that were not working well. Management was about correcting broken processes. Management was about eliminating waste and mistakes. Rarely was there talk of how to bring an organization or its people to exceptionally high levels of performance. An oft-used phrase was "management by exception." Mistakes, problems, and process failures were brought to management.

Then Peter Drucker in the 1950s began to talk about the importance of organizations focusing on people's strengths rather than being preoccupied with their weaknesses. Appendix B chronicles the history of our growing understanding of the important role of strengths in developing leaders.

The Biggest Challenge When Focusing on Strengths

. . . is our seemingly innate desire to fix our weaknesses.

Over the past decade, we have conducted workshops with tens of thousands of leaders. Our message has been consistent. We have urged people to focus on their strengths and to only be concerned with weaknesses when it appears that they are fatal flaws. When the time comes to prepare an individual development plan, we have observed time and time again the tendency for people to gravitate toward correcting a weakness rather than building a strength. Indeed, it seems to happen about 70 percent of the time, even though fatal flaws appear less than 30 percent of the time.

We frequently observe how difficult it is for people to even carefully read through the comments made to them about their strengths. They immediately want to pass these by and move on to read comments that describe whether others perceive them having any potential fatal flaws. And if they don't find that others see them as having fatal flaws, then they quickly delve into the section that comments on what a person in their position needs to do in order to be maximally effective. Those sections appear to hold far greater interest and attraction than the section that dealt with their strengths. Maybe this can be explained by our cultural norm of acting with modesty and humility.

There may be other explanations. But the math suggests that with only 28 percent of leaders having a fatal flaw, the remaining 72 percent of leaders should be focused on building their strengths. By not doing that, this large group is failing to benefit from the advantages of the building-on-strengths approach. Their leadership development efforts may still have an impact, but their effort will be suboptimized. So the biggest challenge in focusing on strengths . . . is our innate desire to fix our weaknesses.

CHAPTER 3

Strengths Can Be Developed

Diverse Ways to Take Your Strengths to the Next Level

When someone learns that your life's work is to develop more effective leaders, the most frequently asked question is something like: "Well, do you really think leaders can be made, or aren't they born that way?" It is fascinating that while the broad question is being asked, there is an implied point of view on the part of the majority. It appears that most questioners lean toward the belief that leaders are indeed born that way. One intriguing dimension of this question is the universality of it. It gets asked in all countries. It has been asked for as long as any of the authors has been living, and presumably for centuries before that. It is recorded that Aristotle once remarked that "some men are born to lead, and others to be led." What's even more interesting, however, is that people of keen intellect and extensive education ask it as frequently as any others. And the question seems for the most part to be absolutely sincere. Normally there are no barbs wrapped around it.

We have not given much recognition to the other side of the question. Those in the leadership development profession have been quick to say, "Leaders are made." A good example of this comes from the well-respected scholar on leadership, Warren Bennis, who wrote:

> The most dangerous leadership myth is that leaders are born—that there is a genetic factor to leadership. Myth asserts that people simply either have certain charismatic qualities or not. That's **nonsense**; in fact, the opposite is true. Leaders are made rather than born.

While we thoroughly agree with Warren Bennis's general conclusion, there is some credible evidence for both sides of the question; and in Appendix A, we present a more thorough answer to this question. At this point, we're going to give the simple answer and say that effective leaders are created through a mixture of "made and born" and that the weight of evidence is clearly on the side of leaders being made.

In our earlier book, *The Extraordinary Leader*, we included a chapter describing how the U.S. Marine Corps approaches the development of leaders. The U.S. Marine Corps has a 220-year track record of successfully doing just that. The Corps' long experience, experimentation, and thoughtfulness have come together to create an extremely effective leadership development system. We have written this new chapter to buttress the argument that leaders can be made. We begin by noting that several corporations have also earned strong reputations for developing leaders. General Electric is known for producing scores of leaders who are continually being recruited away from the company. Most have highly successful careers in leading a variety of other organizations. The same is true of General Mills, Proctor & Gamble and Johnson & Johnson. Such examples attest to the fact that leadership strengths can be developed.

How Strengths Are Developed

The development of strengths is a complex process. We will present an overview in this chapter and then devote the chapters in Part II to the elements of this process. The process involves six elements or stages:

1. Learn the basics
2. Learn through formal development
3. Build in feedback processes
4. Do cross-training
5. Learn while working
6. Create sustainability

1. Learn the Basics

If you concur that leadership is a set of skills and not a body of knowledge or a personality type, then learning leadership skills probably has much in common with learning any other set of skills. Consider the most basic of skills that a child needs to learn. How did you learn to dress yourself or eat food with a knife, fork, and spoon in place of your hands? How does anyone learn these skills? Stanford psychologist Albert Bandura literally wrote the book on this. It is titled *Social Learning Theory* and fundamentally shows that such skills are learned when people observe others. Children mimic their parents. The child watches carefully as the parent shows how to tie shoelaces into a bow, and then the child mimics and practices those actions. We learned most of our skills by watching others perform them, and we then selected those actions that seemed feasible and comfortable for us to duplicate.

We believe the same principle holds true for the acquisition of leadership skills. Young employees in an organization watch how the boss conducts a meeting. They watch how the boss delegates an assignment. They watch how the boss responds to questions regarding the organization's services, or how he or she replies to a question about the firm's products. (This obviously is more relevant and applicable when it relates to the overt, behavioral side of leadership and management. It is harder to observe strategic thinking.)

Much of this learning is casual and informal. It happens at seemingly random times and in short bursts. This process continues on. Some have estimated that possibly 70 percent of what we learn is via this informal process.

2. Learn Through Formal Development

Added to the role of learning through observation is the contribution of more formal development. In some skill areas, such as our use of various applications for the computer, formal classes provide extremely helpful information and jump-start a person's progress. The same holds true for learning leadership skills. New supervisors are often given the opportunity to acquire the leadership skills demanded of an effective first-line leader. Content for formal programs is extremely varied and ranges from specific skills, such as coaching, giving presentations, delegating, doing problem solving, or interviewing, to broader topics, such as understanding emotional intelligence or being more inspirational and motivating.

An extremely powerful formal development process for teaching many leadership skills is behavior modeling. This technology utilizes video clips that show managers handling difficult situations well. The course content explains the key action steps that were being followed. The bulk of the learning process involves participants practicing and rehearsing these skills with one another.

There are several other powerful formal learning methods. These include simulations and action learning projects in which participants tackle challenging opportunities and real problems faced by their organization.

3. Build in Feedback Processes

One way of increasing the value of formal development is to add feedback into the learning experience. This feedback provides people with a clearer picture of their abilities.

CASE STUDY

Paul was an intelligent and talented engineer. He had progressed speedily in his career, moving to senior engineer, project manager, and eventually manager of a group of engineers that supported the company's most profitable product. Paul was viewed as the best-informed and most knowledgeable person in the unit. He loved to involve himself in solving problems and in introducing new technical innovation into the next-generation products. While the performance of Paul's group was good, team members were often very confused about work assignments and never very sure about changes or company direction. Paul had been a manager for over 18 months, and none of his direct reports had ever had a performance discussion. Meetings were haphazard, lacking organization and any agenda. Time was squandered. People rarely felt clear about decisions.

Paul participated in a leadership development program, and a key element of the program was a 360 assessment. As Paul reviewed the results from his 360 assessment, it became apparent that his skills in communicating were rated negatively. Virtually all Paul's respondents rated communicating powerfully as a behavior needing significant improvement. Written comments also identified communication as a a leadership skill needing substantial improvement.

Paul's Plan for Fixing a Fatal Flaw

Paul received the feedback in the same spirit in which it had been given. He created an action plan for improving his communication skills.

Paul's Action Plan

- Hold a team meeting every week to communicate information, review assignments, and share expectations. Create an agenda for important meetings.
- Schedule monthly performance discussions with each direct report.
- E-mail his manager every other week with a progress report on his assignments.
- Schedule a monthly feedback meeting or phone call with every internal customer he and his group served.
- Hold a monthly "lunch-and-learn" session with his team to share best practices, new innovations, and new developments.

Paul stuck to his plan and did all of the above activities faithfully for the next year. He then did a follow-up 360 to check his progress. Paul was pleased, because he moved communication from being a fatal flaw to a behavior that

(continues)

(continued)

was now well above average. Interestingly enough, scores on other leadership skills rose as well, even though he had not made a conscious effort to work on them.

As Paul made significant progress in improving his communication capability, the performance of his group also substantially improved. Paul was personally inspired by the impact of his improved communication on the team. Seeing that progress was so forthcoming, he decided to continue the improved process. If he could move this competency from being a virtual fatal flaw to the point of being well above average, how about moving it from being good to being truly exceptional?

Paul's Plan for Going from Good to Exceptional

Paul's basic assumption about creating a new action plan was that if he increased the frequency of each step, he would continue to increase his effectiveness.

Let us pause for a moment in this description of Paul's quest to become an excellent communicator to ask a key question. Is the way that we successfully fix a weakness the same way we succeed in building a strength? We will continue on with analyzing our case example of Paul to illustrate our point:

Paul's New Action Plan

- Hold a team meeting *twice* per week to communicate information, review assignments, and share expectations. Create an agenda for *every* meeting.

- Schedule *weekly* performance discussions with each direct report.

- E-mail his manager *every week* with a progress report on assignments. In addition, make these reports *more detailed.*

- Schedule a *weekly* feedback meeting with internal customers he and his group served.

- Hold lunch-and-learn sessions *every other week* with his team to share best practices, new innovations, and new developments.

After implementing his new action plan for a month, Paul was surprised to find that the increased frequency was not having a positive effect. In fact, it seemed to be frustrating his direct reports, manager, and customers. It became apparent that what had lifted Paul from a negative position would not lift him to a level of excellence. This would apparently require a different approach.

When Linear Development Runs Out of Gas

Linear development reaches a point of diminishing returns. It invariably runs out of gas when a person has reached a higher level of proficiency.

For example, if a leader wished to increase competence in problem-solving skills, he or she could find a good course on problem-solving techniques or read a book on the overall process. Both the course and the book would probably recommend the following:

- Get immersed in the technology surrounding the problem at hand.

- Define the problem clearly and in a way that increases the likelihood of it being solved.

- Collect information about the problem.

- Explore at least three reasonable alternatives.

- Test each alternative.

- Decide which of these alternatives (or some combination of alternatives) to pursue.

But, frankly, most books on problem solving say much the same thing. Popular courses follow the principles laid out in the books. Not much new has been researched or written in the past few years. Once you've either taken the class or read the books, now what do you do? There are some special problem-solving techniques that can be learned (such as brainstorming or root-cause analysis), but there will quickly come a time when more information will not make the difference.

The process we used to improve a weakness might be described as a linear process. Paul's initial plan was to run straight at the problem. His initial problem was that he did not communicate enough, and so increasing the frequency of his communication had an extremely positive impact.

If a person wants to run a marathon but does not currently run at all, the best training advice is, "Start running." When people go about considering ideas for personal improvement, they often approach the problem using very linear thinking. The good news is that this approach works at getting people to move from poor performance to acceptable performance.

Some strengths of the linear approach are that it is highly efficient and perfectly adapted for learning something new. It also works when a person is coming from a point of deficiency and seeking to move upward. And there is an inherent logic about what is being recommended. Linear development activities have a strong "face validity."

For example, one of the differentiating competencies we identified is that of *develops others*. Following are some linear activities that the manager could initiate:

- Encourage the organization to provide formal training.
- Identify training programs that improve performance and skills.
- Delegate tasks that require people to stretch and acquire new skills and knowledge.
- Invite junior employees to work with senior people on projects.
- Review and refine each person's career plans and development.
- Build the visibility and credibility of junior colleagues by touting their accomplishments to others in the organization.
- Schedule regular coaching sessions with the individual.

It should be obvious that these would all be appropriate for new managers—and also for those with several years under their belt but who had not fully realized the extent of their responsibilities for the development of their people.

4. Do Cross-Training

Cross-training is a type of nonlinear development. It is something that athletes engage in frequently.

The "Why" of Cross-Training

When athletes aspire to become more than just casual participants in a sport, they often turn to cross-training. Aspiring runners take up cycling, swimming, and weight lifting. Tennis players engage in long-distance running and weight lifting. Our favorite example is the football coach who scheduled several of the lumbering linemen to take ballet lessons in an attempt to make them more conscious of their foot-work and to acquire more agility.

What is the underlying reason for cross-training? One way to explain it is that there is a strong, statistically significant correlation between people who are skilled cyclists and those who excel at running. It is always reasonable to ask the "why" question. Athletic trainers and coaches would respond by saying something about the cross-training activity strengthening the muscles used in the other activity, or creating greater aerobic capacity, or building general endurance; or they would give some other logical explanation. But the fundamental explanation is that doing the one has been shown to help people do the other more effectively.

Leadership Cross-Training

As our team was completing the research that identified the six-teen differentiating competencies of the most effective leaders, Joe Folkman walked into Jack Zenger's office and said, "I've found some-thing that you might be interested in. For every one of the differen-tiating competencies, there are a handful of other behaviors that are statistically significantly linked to them. Leaders who got high scores on any competency got high scores on these other behaviors, and the ones that got low scores, got low scores on those same behaviors. Do you find that interesting?"

That was the beginning of this extremely powerful stream of research. We have identified between 5 and 12 companion behaviors for each of the differentiating competencies. The correlations of the companion behaviors to the differentiating competencies are statisti-cally significant. In some cases, the linkage seems rather obvious and reasonable. In other cases, it is rather surprising and nonintuitive.

For example, the companion behaviors to the competency of *practices self-development* are mostly those that describe the leader's involvement with others and their development. These include listening, being open to the ideas of others, respecting others, exhibiting honesty and integrity, and taking the initiative and willingness to risk and challenge the status quo.

The value of these competency companions, from our perspective, is rather simple. For leaders who are already quite skillful at some competency, what is the best way to help them move to the point where this becomes a profound strength? Linear development techniques have, as was suggested earlier, simply run out of gas. These leaders read the book. They've taken the class. They've been to the seminar. Now what?

Competency companions provide a new and more complete pathway to developing a strength. Despite the fact that we may not know the exact reasons for the correlation between the companion behavior and the differentiating competency, it is still true that a person that gets a high score on one tends to also get a high score on the other. This suggests that pulling the score up on the one will have a high likelihood of bringing the score up on the other.

Developing Strengths Is a Different Process from Correcting a Weakness

We have noted that developing a strength invariably demands greater involvement and commitment on the part of the participant than fixing a weakness. With practice and effort it is a straightforward process to move from "poor" performance to "good" performance. The above case of Paul is an excellent example. To make the transition from "good" to "great" is much more difficult primarily because the level of skill needs to be distinctively better. That is illustrated in the realm of physical health. If someone has contracted a case of pneumonia, a physician can treat it with antibiotics and help the patient get well. Drugs can help rid the lungs of the contaminated fluid, and so the person can move toward greater health. But getting ready to run a 10K race, a half marathon, or a triathlon event is a whole different matter. This entails dramatically different activities, all of which demand a far higher level of dedication, involvement, and sheer hard work.

5. Learn While Working

Strengths may also be developed by deliberately creating opportunities for improving our skills through practice in the normal course of daily work. Having once identified a strength to be enhanced, a leader who is serious about developing that strength will find opportunities to practice that behavior.

One of the sixteen differentiating competencies we identified was *develops strategic perspective*. Virtually all leaders can view their roles from a longer-term and broader perspective. This may necessitate talking with others in the organization who may have a better window into both the past and the future of the organization, as well as those who have demonstrated their ability to create a distinctive vision for their part of the organization or who have better insight into the competitors. Every leader can find ways to obtain customers' perspectives on the products and services the organization provides, an approach that has been shown to greatly enhance strategic perspective.

6. Create Sustainability

It is one thing to acquire a new skill or to enhance one already possessed. But how do we keep this skill alive and growing? This final step in building a strength is the one that locks this strength into place. Sustainability and follow-through come from:

- Creating a supportive environment from manager(s), peers, and subordinates

- Providing clearly defined outcomes for the development
- Establishing well-defined accountability and responsibility for participants' implementing and applying what they learn
- Building systems that provide visibility
- Implementing various methods of follow-up, such as additional sessions, telephone calls, and accountability partners within the organization

The Special Challenge of Leadership Skills

The realm of developing leadership skills includes one special challenge. The great majority of leaders in organizations begin their careers in some area of specialty. The leader may have been a chemist, an accountant, a marketer, an operations manager, an IT specialist, or a lawyer. The technical education of these leaders was usually focused in their area of specialty. Their career aspirations were most often to excel in the career of their choice. Many wanted to be the best possible chemical engineer, or software programmer, or whatever their career choice had been.

But in all likelihood, most never gave much thought to the idea that "as my career progresses, I will shift my aspirations away from my technical specialty to becoming an exceptional leader." The need to acquire a high level of leadership skills is usually an afterthought and comes at a later point in their career development.

Their leadership skills have been acquired by observing and mimicking the bosses they've had to-date. There may have been some formal development experiences, but in most organizations these are relatively minimal. Worse yet, only 37 percent of companies that have an average of 35,000 employees have any ongoing leadership development programs. This suggests that in the large majority of firms, leadership development programs are either unavailable or very sporadic.

This makes it rather difficult for leaders to quickly and efficiently acquire the skills required to perform at an adequate level. Often, depending on their area of specialty, leaders continue to spend a good part of their day in the technical area in which they were trained, and only a portion of their day is spent in leadership activities.

If they're lucky, they will have had some outstanding role models from which to learn. But if they are like the great majority of people in organizations, those role models will have been few in number and far between. Our informal surveys of managers confirm that, at best, most can only think of one or two bosses whom they have considered to be outstanding leaders. Many have never had one.

How can competent individual contributors learn leadership skills, and how do good leaders become great leaders? We are optimistic that great leaders can be developed, but in order to do so, the development process needs to move beyond the prevailing linear logic.

Developing Strengths Is More Successful Than Correcting Weaknesses

Here are some hard data that shed light on this important finding. We conducted a study following an organization's 360 survey process in which we separated those leaders who elected to work on developing their weaknesses from those who worked primarily on developing their strengths. Figure 3.1 tells an important story. Some 12 to 18 months following the initial 360 survey and development efforts of the participating leaders, we repeated the 360 and development process. This allowed for sufficient time to lapse for new and changed leadership behaviors to be visible. The repeat 360 enabled us to measure improvement or gain over time—if there was any. If weaknesses can't be improved or if strengths can't be magnified, then the results of the two tests should be relatively identical.

Figure 3.1 Building Strengths Produces Superior Outcomes

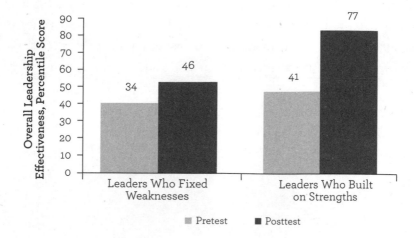

Note that both groups got better. We think this is extremely positive news, and it supports the wisdom of organizations investing in their leaders. Weaknesses get in people's way and detract from their effectiveness, as we noted in Chapter 2. The results clearly indicate that these weaknesses can be improved. Also note, however, that the group who focused on strengths showed three times the improvement as those working on weaknesses.

In our earlier book, *The Extraordinary Leader,* we discovered that it was the presence of strengths and not the absence of weaknesses that created exceptional leaders. This strength-building approach has fundamentally changed the way many organizations go about developing their leaders. By focusing on strengths rather than on weaknesses, organizations have created a more positive approach to development, and at the same time they have increased the leadership effectiveness of executives, managers, and individual contributors. For leaders to develop strengths, they need to utilize a nonlinear approach. Taking advantage of leadership cross-training makes strength-building possible. By measuring leaders who have gone through this development process, we have proven that leaders can significantly improve their ability to lead others. The evidence is clear that organizations taking advantage of this process will achieve greater improvement. We have also found that utilizing formal learning, feedback from others, cross-training, learning while working, and sustaining the process with follow-up significantly enhances the learning and development of leaders.

Leadership Cross-Training

The Revolutionary Approach to Developing Leadership Skills

Can Leadership Skills Be Acquired?

Nearly every discipline has its areas of disagreement and conflict. In the world of leadership development, one of the most deep-rooted conflicts occurs between two groups: those who believe that leadership is the result of talents that only some people possess and those who believe that leadership skills can be acquired. We have observed that even among the first group—those who emphasize the importance of talents—there are shades of opinion. Some believe these talents are largely genetically determined. Even more believe that such talents are largely in place by the time a person finishes the teenage years; they seem less sure that leaders are hardwired at birth, but they are insistent that once a person reaches the age of 20, behaviors, attitudes, traits, and abilities are largely settled into place and that not much change will occur.

The countervailing position seems obvious. While understanding that a great deal of molding and shaping occurs in those early years, the second group is much more optimistic about people's ability to change and develop. This latter group recognizes that many people do seem cemented in their ways, but the group contends that some people simply do not seek to change and improve. In addition, we are constantly finding new and better ways to help people learn and grow, and part of the phenomenon of people being stuck in ruts after the age of 20 has been our lack of better ways to help them progress and evolve upward in skills. If it is not already obvious to the reader, let us clearly go on record as saying that we are in the second camp.

How Leaders Can Grow and Develop Throughout Their Entire Career

We now want to introduce you to a unique part of our research— research that supports the argument that strengths can indeed be developed. Several colleagues who are well versed in the field of leadership development have told us that this may well be the most important of our contributions to the field. We believe that it represents a fresh, new approach to help leaders develop strengths. It rounds out the spectrum of tools available to the leader.

Our definition of linear development encompasses those activities that are logical, obvious approaches for an individual to improve. If people realize that they are not highly strategic in their thinking, then linear development would have them read books about strategy, take classes, subscribe to journals, volunteer to participate in the strategic planning process for their group, and spend time with those in the organization who are perceived as being particularly good strategic thinkers.

Such activities, however, quickly reach a point of diminishing returns. They simply run out of gas when a person has reached a higher level of proficiency. Assume that someone has learned the basics and practiced them. The person has placed herself into situations in which she can receive feedback that would help her correct any problems and advance even further. But she reaches a plateau. She senses her development has stopped, but she does not know what else to do.

For example, if a leader wished to increase her problem-solving skills, she could find a good course on problem-solving techniques or read a book on the technique. The course would most likely talk about:

- Identifying a problem
- Collecting information about it
- Carefully defining the problem
- Describing a satisfactory solution
- Implementing creative techniques for increasing divergent thinking
- Generating alternative solutions
- Selecting the criteria by which a final solution will be chosen
- Selecting a final solution
- Planning for its implementation
- Holding a final debrief session to capture what was learned in the process

But, frankly, most books on this topic say much the same thing. And most courses follow the principles laid out in the books. We are not aware that much new has been researched or written in the past few years. Once you've either taken the class or read a couple of the books, now what do you do? There may be some specific techniques that can be learned (brainstorming or root-cause analysis), but there will quickly come a time when more information will not make the difference.

The "Why" of Cross-Training How Leadership Cross-Training Works

This brings us to the concept of leadership cross-training. Most of us are familiar with the basic concept of cross-training, and we touched on it in Chapter 3. A person who aspires to be a serious runner concludes that there are only a certain number of miles that she can run per week. After reading magazines and talking to other accomplished runners, she decides to engage in a series of other activities such as weight lifting, bicycle riding, and swimming. Other runners have chosen to do rowing and water aerobics. Why? Because people who engage in these other activities have found that they help them to run better, to be in better physical condition, to gain aerobic capacity, and not to be as prone to incur injury that would come from only running. Beyond that, this variety of activities makes the time spent in physical activity go by more rapidly and even more enjoyably.

Cross-training is an optimum solution for someone who is reasonably good at something and who wants to continue excelling at it and then to move into the higher ranks in any given activity or sport.

CASE STUDY IN CROSS-TRAINING

Dave is the manager of an organization's research and development unit. He is by nature an introvert. He is not an active contributor in most meetings. When he participates, his comments are offered with some hesitation, almost an apology. In past meetings with customers and representatives from other departments, there had been occasional comments questioning his technical competence and the reason for his being in this position. Does he really belong in this job? Specifically, on a recent 360-degree feedback instrument, he was given feedback regarding his level of technical competence that indicated that some peers had questions about his knowledge regarding the firm's technology.

Upon reading this, Dave decided to take this feedback to heart. His knee-jerk response was that this should be fairly easy to fix. Just bump up the level of knowledge about the firm's technology so that he could answer every question and never be stumped with anything tossed at him.

Dave began looking at his library of books in his office. He had virtually every important book dealing with the firm's technology right there on his shelf. He had just received a catalog from the local university describing extension courses in his field. After scanning the list, he was aware that he either had taken many of them or was more technically qualified than the instructors for the few classes he had not taken. He thought about the annual trade conference at which technical sessions would be offered. He went online to review the agenda for this year's conference. Nothing looked all that promising or helpful.

Then Dave recalled that as part of the 360-degree feedback process, the facilitator had talked about a different approach to developing important competencies. She had called that new approach "nonlinear development." He recalled talk of cross-training and how the best way to develop some important skills may well be to build around them and not run straight into the headwind.

(continues)

(continued)

Dave got out his manual and looked at this specific competency of technical competence. After examining the behaviors that described this competency, and after reviewing some fairly obvious, straightforward remedies, he decided to plow on to the next section. He smiled, because all the things he'd been contemplating were very linear. This included such steps as "read more more books and articles" and "attend technical conventions"—all those were obvious and completely linear.

As Dave looked at the next section in the manual, an interesting solution suddenly caught his eye. He thought, "That may be it—the thing I need to change." We will continue to examine Dave's situation later in the chapter.

Correlations Between Competencies and Other Behaviors

As we conducted our original research on leadership competencies, an interesting fact emerged. For every differentiating competency such as *drives for results, solves problems and analyzes issues, takes initiative, communicates powerfully and prolifically, innovates, engages in collaboration and teamwork,* and *inspires and motivates others to high performance,* there were a handful of behaviors whose correlations with each competency were statistically significant. A person who received high scores on a specific differentiating competency also received high scores on several behaviors, and a person receiving low scores on that differentiating competency would invariably receive low scores on those same behaviors. It was as if they were bound together.

Might this discovery provide some insight into how those who aspired to develop a strength could better achieve this strength? This concept has been featured in an article that two of this book's coauthors wrote for *Harvard Business Review*, titled, "Make Yourself Indispensable," published in October 2011.

The Interaction Effect

As we began to better understand the interplay of these competencies, we noticed that there were strong interaction effects when leaders performed two competencies well. To understand this interaction effect, we looked at the probability of a leader being at the 90th percentile in overall leadership effectiveness. We first examined the impact of one competency when it was a strength at the 75th percentile and the effect of combining it with others that were below the 75th percentile. The two that we analyzed were *has technical or professional expertise* and *communicates powerfully and prolifically*. Figure 4.1 shows the individual effects ("A without B" and "B without A") and the interaction effect ("Both A and B").

What we started to understand was that profound strengths are created from the combination of competencies. The following question and answer became quite clear:

Q: What is better than a leader who has deep technical or professional expertise?

Figure 4.1 What Happens When You Combine Competencies

Competency A	A without B	Competency B	B without A	Both A and B
Has technical/ professional expertise	3%	Communicates powerfully and prolifically	14%	82%

> A: A leader who has deep technical or professional expertise *and* who also is able to communicate and share that expertise with others in a powerful way.

Technical expertise without powerful communications is much like a great professor who teaches as a mime would (i.e., great knowledge but incomplete communication).

The research helped us understand that a profound strength is created by taking one competency that has moderately good scores and combining that skill with another competency. The combination of the two skills creates an effect that is greater than the effect of either skill individually. As we explored these powerful combinations, we discovered that many of them were associated with each competency. We called these powerful combinations *companion competencies*. We reasoned that if we could map out which companion competencies created the most powerful combinations, that map could provide leaders with better guidance about how to create a profound strength in any competency. Many of the combined effects were not intuitively obvious. The only way to truly uncover the companion competencies was by data-mining huge data sets of 360 assessments.

Intuitive and Nonintuitive Companion Competencies

One of the fascinating characteristics of these companion competencies was the fact that some were extremely logical and intuitive. On the other hand, many were jarringly nonintuitive. It was hard to find a rationale for some of them being so highly correlated with each other. Such is the beauty of relying on empirical data. You go where it leads you and ask questions later.

For example, one of our differentiating competencies is a leader's ability to practice self-development. When we ask people to predict the behaviors that would correlate with this competency, people offer such ideas as taking courses, reading books, and setting personal goals for development. That would have been our assumption as well.

Empirically, the behaviors most correlated with *practices self-development* were:

- Listens
- Is open to ideas from others
- Shows respect for others
- Displays integrity
- Avoids taking credit for others' success
- Desires to develop others
- Takes initiative
- Is willing to take risks and to challenge the status quo

What we find so fascinating about this list is that the first six items, which also happened to be those most highly correlated with the differentiating competency, were items having to do with the relationship of the leader with other people. They were not self-focused, nor were they inwardly focused. Apparently, being perceived as practicing self-development has much more to do with how a leader interacts with others than how many books the leader reads or classes he or she takes.

Using Companion Competencies for Leadership Development

Let's go back to Dave. Dave wanted to be perceived as being thoroughly technically competent. His organization is a large, nationally respected IT company. A special competency companion analysis had been done for that organization. As Dave examined the research on companion competencies for technical and professional expertise in his organization, his eye was drawn to three of the most statistically linked companion competencies:

- Solving problems
- Relationship building and networking
- Communication and influence skills

Immediately Dave had a flash of insight. In his normal interactions with others in the organization, he kept to himself. He didn't reach out to others. His friends kidded him about his isolationist behavior. His boss had alluded to this in performance reviews. His excuse had always been, "That's who I am." But the fact of the matter was that he did not have an extensive network of colleagues with whom he had lunch or any other social connections. That was clearly something he could do better.

So what's the link with how he is perceived technically? Our guess is that people seek answers from those they know best. They call someone whom they feel is a friend. Dave was not the person who came to mind as a friend.

In meetings, Dave was not a frequent contributor. He responded when people asked him a question, but his answers were terse and to the point. He prided himself on Calvin Coolidge brevity. He didn't elaborate or go behind the question to see if his answers satisfied what people really wanted to know. His wife frequently pointed this out to him, and Dave could see that maybe he could improve how he was perceived by reaching out and speaking up—certainly this seemed a much more likely solution than reading additional books and journals and attending conferences and seminars.

Even though Dave sees the need for improving his communication skills, there is the possibility that he may lack the desire and passion to improve. And without the passion to improve, the result might not change much. The variety of different companion competencies provides a number of different options for people to improve a competency. If communication and influence skills are not a fatal flaw, then Dave may choose another companion behavior for improving his technical expertise. He may find he has more passion and energy for problem solving as another way to demonstrate his expertise. One of the best ways to show others the depth of your expertise is to solve a difficult problem or come up with a new solution. Given Dave's situation and his personal passion, using a companion competency can provide a variety of options for every person to build his or her strengths.

Another illustration may help to fully grasp this point:

One of the most frequent developmental targets that we see is the one having to do with developing strategic perspective. Chances are we've all heard some colleague dinged by others because he wasn't "strategic in his thinking." The frustrating thing about that specific piece of feedback is that people's definitions of strategic thinking differ so widely from one another. We suspect that strategic thinking generally refers to a person's ability to think in the big picture, and that takes into account what is happening in the industry as well as in the broader economy. It also usually refers to an ability to take a longer-term view rather than being immersed in what's happening tomorrow or next month. But what develops strategic thinking in people?

A few of the companion competencies to strategic thinking are fascinating. They are:

- Customer focus

- Innovation

- Problem solving

Again, we confess that if we had predicted what would be on this list, these are not the ones we would have come up with. So what might explain this interesting trio? The more we have pondered this, the more that *customer focus* makes sense. Customers' wants and needs drive a business, and organizations that are best in tune with customers are those that succeed.

In coaching conversations with numerous leaders over the years, we have made the specific recommendation of visiting customers and stressed the importance of doing this. Many have come back and thanked us for our encouragement to get out of their offices and make such visits. They believed, in hindsight, that it was some of the most valuable time they spent. Most could readily see how it would help them to be more strategic in their thinking.

What's the link between strategic thinking and *innovation*? It makes little sense to engage in strategic thinking and planning if you are not a person who is extremely eager and willing to try new things. Plus the strategic thinking process demands a willingness to be open to new and different approaches. Dyer, Gregerson, and Christensen have written about innovation in the *Harvard Business Review* and in their book *The Innovators's DNA*.[1] They concluded that one of the key reasons why some executives are so effective in leading their organizations to new heights has to do with a high level of innovativeness, which comes from asking penetrating questions, being astute observers, and being willing to experiment. By doing these things, they guide their organizations in a highly strategic fashion through the minefields in the competitive landscape.

Correlation and Cross-Training

One way of viewing cross-training is to simply acknowledge that those activities that athletes use for their cross-training are those that have been shown to have a high correlation with the skill they seek to acquire. A high level of proficiency in swimming is strongly correlated with high proficiency in running. A high level of proficiency in bicycling is positively correlated with a high proficiency in running, and the same for rowing or weight lifting.

Developing Humility

One of our clients wanted to measure and develop the capabilities of their leaders on a competency the company called "humility." This quality had been emphasized by Jim Collins and discussed in his book *Good to Great*. Humility is a difficult skill to personally assess. People who think they have humility oftentimes don't. We were able to create a very predictive measure of humility, but our next problem was helping leaders develop and improve on this skill. It is difficult to come up with a plan for improving humility, and often leaders would write something like "Just be more humble" or "Don't be arrogant." Many people believed that the absence of arrogance created humility. Those were obviously not useful action plans.

Put yourself in the shoes of a leader who receives feedback that he is above average in humility but he very much wants this to be a profound strength. What might be your action plan for making humility a profound strength?

- Be more self-effacing
- Make self-deprecating remarks
- Speak softly
- Be more tentative in comments
- Ask for other's opinions before giving own

Do you feel that if you executed your action plan, you would make a significant improvement in your humility?

Most people doing this exercise come up short. It is almost impossible to figure out what you could do to improve. One person did come up with a development plan that we thought would work. The suggestion was, "Join a monastery and give up all my earthly possessions." But since only a select few people are willing to join a monastery, perhaps we need to look at a different approach.

Competency Companions for Humility

We decided the best way to build humility was to study people who are perceived as humble and identify more specifically what they do. Using 360 assessment data, we identified a large group of people who were rated by others on their display of humility. By mining this data set, we were able to identify a set of companion competencies. From our research, eight companion competencies merged:

1. Has concern and consideration for others
2. Values diversity and inclusion
3. Shows assertiveness
4. Is open to feedback
5. Has integrity
6. Develops others
7. Involves others
8. Is personally accountable

These companion competencies provided powerful insights on specific actions that leaders could take to be more humble.

Possible Rationale for Companion Competencies to Humility

The following is an explanation for how each of the companion competencies may impact and influence a person's humility.

1. *Has concern and consideration for others.* Leaders who were humble were much more effective at showing concern for other people. Leaders who lacked humility tended to be perceived as caring only for themselves.

2. *Values diversity and inclusion.* There was a strong connection between being a leader who valued differences and appreciated diversity and being perceived as humble.

3. *Shows assertiveness.* This was a real surprise. Our assumption about humble leaders was that they were meek and mild, but the research showed strong correlations to assertiveness. Truly humble leaders are willing to take a stand and put things right. Humility needs to be demonstrated with action. Thanking people for their contribution takes assertiveness, as does admitting when you are wrong.

4. *Is open to feedback.* This companion competency is fairly self-evident. Being open to feedback is a very effective way to demonstrate humility. Resisting or rationalizing feedback is a great way to demonstrate arrogance.

5. *Has integrity.* Having the ability to be totally honest about what really happened even when you are at fault is a wonderful way to show you are humble.

6. *Develops others.* Taking the time to coach, mentor, or teach someone else a new skill shows humility. Getting angry or upset with people when they don't know how to effectively perform their job shows arrogance.

7. *Involves others.* A person who dominates conversations and rarely asks others for their input and ideas is never viewed as humble. Taking the time to truly consider others' ideas and being open to input from others demonstrates humility.

8. *Is personally accountable.* Truly humble people never finger-point when thing go wrong. They accept responsibility.

Companion Competencies and Their Impact on Action Plans

Excellent action plans are difficult to create. The following experience was related by one of the authors about this issue:

Several years ago after running a feedback session with a leader, I asked to see the action plan of one of the participants in the session. The participant pointed to his head and said, "It's all up here."

I then ask what issues he was going to improve. He looked at me and said boldly, "Communication!"

I then said, "What's your plan?"

His reply, "Communicate more."

I asked him, "When?"

His reply was, "All the time."

At this point I gave up and said, "Good luck."

The problem with most development plans is that people just don't know what to do to improve. This is where the companion competencies can make a huge difference. They provide some connections between the competency being developed and other specific behaviors.

READER'S EXERCISE

After reviewing the eight companion competencies associated with humility, think about your own situation and which of these companion competencies would help you to be viewed as more humble. Now select the three or four companion competencies and write an action plan, identifying specific actions you would take to build this strength.

Companion competencies: _____

_____

_____

Action plan: _____

_____

_____

Your Action Plan for Making Humility a Profound Strength

As leaders have utilized the competency companion research, they have quickly come to the conclusion that it provides them with exceptional insight into how they can build a strength. The key for a leader to make the transition from "good" to "great" is strength development. Many times, leaders who have profound strengths are not self-aware about specifically what they do that enables them to have these strengths. If you ask leaders who are humble if their assertiveness or their ability to develop others helped them to be perceived as more humble, most would not see the connection; and frankly we did not see the connection until the data showed the connection. A variety of different approaches, support materials, and guides are available to help people fix weaknesses. This is the only approach available for building strengths. In future chapters, we will show the impact of this approach and the value it creates in organizations.

Why Companion Competencies Work

We don't know. No one knows. That's the honest answer. The exact reasons for the connection between the companion competencies and the differentiating competency are hard to empirically discover. You can measure their correlation, but that doesn't answer the "why" question.

We have several theories that may help in thinking about that question, however:

1. The competency companion may be a "building block" for the competency.

    Example: Focusing on self-development helps leaders better develop others. As I learn to develop myself, it gives me both insight and encouragement to develop my subordinates. But also the things I learn to do in developing myself are some of the things I need to do to develop others.

2. A high level of skill in the companion competencies increases the skill in the competency.

   Example: The ability to integrate information is a companion to *solves problems and analyzes issues.* Integrating information is part of the problem-solving process.

   Example: Establishes stretch goals is a companion competency to *engages in collaboration and teamwork.* These both require some of the same activities and skills.

3. The competency companion helps others "see" the main competency. It is an enabling activity and a conduit by which others can better see the leader's true ability to use the differentiating competency.

   Example: Improved communication helps others see leaders sharing their technical and professional expertise.

   Example: Involving others is a companion competency to *communicates powerfully and prolifically.* Listening expands the communication channel and creates the vehicle by which communication is improved.

The Paradox of Correlation and Causation

Yet every beginning student of statistics learns one axiom, and it is this: simply because things are correlated, that does not necessarily prove that one causes the other. If A and B are correlated with each other, that may be because A causes B, or it may be that B causes A, or it may be that there is still a third element C that causes them both. We understand that logic and the caution about jumping to the conclusion of one thing causing another to occur.

However, we can't ignore the fact that much of science begins by someone noting that two things go together. The statistical correlation between smoking and lung cancer finally brought this forcefully to the attention of the world. In the early years after the correlation was identified, cigarette company executives attempted to deny the conclusion that smoking caused lung cancer. Today, few would deny that smoking causes lung cancer, and it was the statistical correlation that led researchers to this fact.

Often, when two things go together, it is fairly obvious which one causes the other or if they are caused by something else. It is a fact that girls who watch soap operas have more eating disorders than those who don't. Regardless of your opinion of the acting, the story line, or the plot of daytime soap operas, chances are that not many believe that the mere act of watching soap operas gives young girls anorexia or bulimia. Most assume that people attracted to daytime soap operas have dimensions to their personality that are linked to eating disorders. People who own red cars are twice as likely to be involved in traffic accidents as those owning blue cars. So if I own a red car and paint it blue, will I be less apt to have an accident? Probably not, because it was the personality characteristics and behavior of the person who bought the red car that is likely to be the main force in being more accident prone.

Maybe both elements are highly correlated because each impacts the other. Statistically, married people are generally happier than those who are single, but it is also true that happier people tend to get married. So being happy and being married may have a tendency to elevate the other, and it is impossible to determine which comes first. (And we all know lots of exceptions to this statistical generalization.)

Even in nature, when we see two events occurring together, it is somewhat obvious why one would cause the other. There is a high correlation between ice cream consumption and shark attacks. But no rational person believes that either of these causes the other. Both are obviously tied to the temperature. Another example is crickets chirping and the temperature. At higher temperatures, crickets chirp more frequently. At colder temperatures, crickets chirp less frequently. We suspect most observers would conclude that it is the change in temperature that causes crickets to vary their speed of chirping—and that it is not how fast the crickets chirp that causes the temperature to rise.

A Final Thought

We offer one final comment about using competency companions. We have observed that people often get stuck. And because they don't know exactly what to do, they end up doing nothing. Yet doing something is usually better than doing nothing (as long as it isn't absolutely the wrong thing). Companion competencies open the door of people's thinking and give them a fresh avenue to pursue. Because of the high, positive statistical correlation, we're reasonably confident that pursuing a companion competency is the right thing to do. But if nothing else, at the very least it gives the person hope and encouragement to do something. Because competencies are so highly interconnected, the fact that the individual is doing something has high odds of producing a favorable outcome.

Benefits from Developing Strengths

Why Focusing on Weaknesses Doesn't Create Exceptional Leadership

Improving leadership effectiveness always has a positive payoff regardless of how it is done. Most leaders are conditioned to use the traditional approach of fixing weaknesses to improve their leadership ability. Increasingly, more leaders are shifting to a strengths-based approach of leadership development in order to raise their effectiveness. In this chapter, we examine the additional payoffs that result when leaders focus on building strengths.

Philosophy of Improvement

Most leaders have a philosophy about personal improvement. This philosophy is rarely explicit but easily recognizable when people go about creating a personal improvement plan. The most common philosophy centers on improving weaknesses. If a leader had a goal of building his or her overall leadership effectiveness to the 70th percentile, the actions for improvement might look as follows:

Improving weakness

Identify strengths and weaknesses. Once the most negative weakness is identified, then work hard to improve that weakness. Eventually evaluate your skills again, and once again work on the most negative item. Over time, by improving all your weaknesses on every competency, you will eventually achieve the 70th percentile.

The implicit assumption of this philosophy is that in order to be highly effective, all the competencies need to be improved. To some extent, people might assume that they can only be as effective as their least positive competency. The lowest competency sets the bar for their personal effectiveness. Over the years, many of the leaders we have worked with have expressed concern that if they don't work on a negative issue, other people will notice and perceive them as not listening to the feedback from others.

Obsessed with Weaknesses

There is a psychological problem that some people experience called *body dysmorphic disorder,* sometimes referred to as *imagined ugliness.* People with this disorder exaggerate a small flaw in their appearance and perceive themselves to be completely ugly or grotesque. They cannot stop thinking about this minor or imagined flaw. They obsess over their body image, and this can consume many hours each day. Some choose to undergo numerous expensive cosmetic surgery procedures in an attempt to correct this disorder, but as could be predicted, such corrective procedures will never cause them to feel satisfied about their appearance.

In many ways, believing that a small weakness will crater a person's overall effectiveness is a similar serious misperception. In talking with groups about strengths and weaknesses, we often ask the groups to think of the best leader that they have ever worked with, know of, or read about. After describing this leader's profound strengths, we ask the question, "Did this leader have any weaknesses?" Almost everyone says yes; and when we ask people to describe what the weakness was, we are frequently surprised to hear things like:

- "He would occasionally lose his temper."
- "This leader was very shortsighted."
- "She failed to appreciate other people."
- "He did not understand the technology."

When asked why the weaknesses did not hurt the leaders, the reply is always the same, though expressed in slightly different words. The message is because their strengths are so profound.

In our experience, if the issues are not "fatal flaws," then people will not overreact to them. If a leader receives feedback and makes an effort to improve, others will be impressed.

Building Strengths

The philosophy of building strengths suggests that leaders ought to find a way to stand out and differentiate themselves. Others will notice our abilities, not our disabilities. If a leader used the building-strength philosophy, the actions for going about improving might look as follows:

Building strength

If I don't have a fatal flaw, then I am free to select any issue for development. My goal is to develop one or two competencies into profound strengths. Since I can choose any competency, I will select those that I feel will have the greatest impact and for which I have a passion for improvement.

Using the building-strength philosophy, an individual selects competencies for improvement in areas that they enjoy and that will have the greatest impact. Following is a description of two leaders' different approaches for development. We invite you to determine which of these two leaders will be more successful in efforts to improve.

Leader A

Leader A selects a competency for improvement on an issue he generally dislikes. His current skill level in this area is acceptable, but it is his lowest-rated competency, and he is embarrassed by the low rating. He feels obligated to work on this competency even though it is not something he enjoys or feels will help him much in his current job. He creates an action plan that is detailed and well organized but feels it is laborious to implement.

Leader B

Since leader B does not have any fatal flaws, she looks over the competencies and asks the question, "Which of these competencies do I enjoy the most? What do I love to do?" She selects four competencies. The next question she asks herself is, "Which of the four competencies if improved would have the greatest impact on my ability to be successful in my current job?" One competency stands out. She creates a plan that looks challenging but fun.

Which leader is going to make the most progress? The answer seems extremely obvious. In spite of this, we observe that roughly two-thirds of leaders continue to make the same decision as leader A.

Evidence for the correctness of leader B's decision is reinforced by a study of leaders working on building strengths or fixing weaknesses.

Impact of Building Strengths

A group of 68 executives went through a 360 development process and were introduced to the concept of building on their strengths rather than fixing weaknesses. Six months after the initial training program where they had selected an issue for development, the executives were surveyed and asked if they had chosen to build on their strengths or fix a weakness. The majority of the executives, 88 percent, indicated they had decided to build on strength, while 12 percent were focused on a weakness. It is interesting how the decision to build on strengths or fix weaknesses impacted their efforts to improve. Table 5.1 shows the percentage of people responding positively.

Table 5.1   How Building on Strengths or
Fixing Weaknesses Impacted Efforts to Improve

Executives Responded to These Statements	People Who Responded Positively	
	Build Strength	Fix Weakness
I have created an excellent development plan that will guide my efforts to improve.	63%	13%
As a result of my use of the 360 feedback process, report, and tools, I feel that I have improved in my overall leadership effectiveness.	72%	38%
I feel that I have moved forward on improving the specific issues on my development plan.	68%	43%
I have taken the time and made a real effort to work on my development plan.	60%	38%

Table 5.1 demonstrates that those leaders who worked on strengths were more likely to:

- Create an excellent development plan
- Improve their overall leadership effectiveness
- Improve specific issues in their development plan
- Allocate appropriate time to development
- Put forth a concerted effort to work on their development plan

The executives were also asked to estimate the impact of their change efforts on business results and on employee commitment. Again the data clearly showed that those who were focused on building their strengths indicated their efforts for change had a much greater impact, as shown in Table 5.2.

Table 5.2 How Building on Strengths or
Fixing Weaknesses Impacted Efforts to Improve

Executives Responded to These Statements	People Who Responded Positively	
	Build Strength	Fix Weakness
My leadership improvement efforts had a positive impact on the business results of my team/organization.	72%	38%
My leadership development efforts had a positive impact on the commitment level of my direct reports.	47%	25%

This study supports the conclusion that there is a significant motivational difference between people who work on strengths and those who work to fix weaknesses. This motivational difference, in turn, has a substantial impact on their level of success.

Results That Come from Building Strengths

One year after the study mentioned above, each of the leaders in the group participated in a follow-up 360 assessment. The follow-up survey asked managers, peers, direct reports, and others the same questions on the same competencies as the pretest assessment. When the original results (pretest) were compared with the follow-up results (posttest), it was discovered that 70 percent of the participants had made some improvement as perceived by those who worked with them. The results for this group were analyzed to identify those leaders who made improvements on strengths versus leaders who made improvements on weaknesses. We wanted to understand the differences in how much progress various leaders made on their improvement efforts. We eliminated those leaders who were rated at the 80th percentile or higher in the pretest results because their ability to show substantial progress was significantly restricted. Figure 5.1 shows the percentile scores for overall leadership effectiveness, comparing pretest and posttest results for leaders who were building strengths versus those fixing weaknesses. For the group fixing weaknesses, we eliminated those who were working to fix fatal flaws (competencies at or below the 10th percentile).

Figure 5.1 Improvement of Overall Leadership Effectiveness

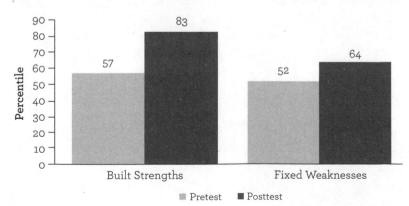

These results are promising and positive because both groups show significant improvements. We know that leaders who attempt to improve their weaknesses can make significant progress. It is fascinating that the group that focused on building strengths improved by 26 percentile points compared with 12 for the group focused on fixing weaknesses. We have seen this effect in multiple studies. Leaders who focus on strengths invariably show more substantial gains.

Outcomes from Improved Leadership Effectiveness

Our studies have confirmed over and over again the relationship between the effectiveness of leaders and the engagement, satisfaction, and commitment of their direct reports. Figure 5.2 compares the pretest versus posttest results of employee engagement, satisfaction, and commitment. The building-strengths group showed an improvement of 12 percentile points, whereas the group that was focused on fixing weaknesses achieved a gain of only 6 percentile points.

This is a very important finding, because it validates the impact of improving leadership capability. In Chapter 1, we outlined the impact

Figure 5.2   Employee Engagement, Satisfaction, and Commitment

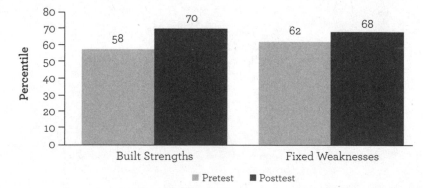

of leadership on a variety of bottom-line outcomes such as employee engagement, customer satisfaction, turnover, and sales. The conclusion of that chapter was that the better the leader, the better the results. This study shows that whatever the starting point, improving leadership behavior leads to improved results.

Benefits of Building on Strengths

There are a variety of benefits that come from building strengths:

1. People are more motivated when they work on their strengths. It will come as no surprise that when people work on something they enjoy, they are more willing to invest time and effort into improvement.

2. Those who worked on their strengths were more successful in their change efforts, and that substantially increased their overall leadership effectiveness.

3. Change in outcomes—such as employee commitment, intention to stay, highly committed employees, total sales, and performance ratings—followed improvement in leadership effectiveness.

4. Such improvement provides incentive and motivation for further development.

The last benefit is best illustrated by the following story:

A few years ago, one of the authors was having an end-of-the-day debrief discussion with David Spong. David was a successful executive with Boeing. He had moved his part of the organization forward in profitability, efficiency, and quality. Two different organizations he led were able to win the coveted Baldrige Award at Boeing. In the discussion, David was asked if the key to leadership improvement was that leaders find and address the one right issue that needed improvement. David restated the question by saying, "Is the key to improvement finding the one right issue that needs to be changed?" After taking a few moments to consider his reply, he then said:

> I think that what is important is that a leader does something—anything—to improve. Perhaps a few leaders need to address a specific issue, but I see leaders who expend all their energy trying to find that one right issue for improvement and who never get around to doing anything. If a leader selects an issue that they can make progress on and that moves them forward, then my experience is that this improvement will make a positive difference in their team. Doing something is much better than doing nothing.

Building strengths increases the likelihood that leaders will do something.

How Exceptional Strengths Are Developed

This section of the book is its heart. While it requires some effort to discover your strengths, the real challenge is how to escalate a competency you possess that is hovering now at the 65th percentile up to the 90th percentile.

The following chapters build on Chapter 4 and the concept of non-linear development, or cross-training. This philosophy pervades many of the developmental processes outlined in these successive chapters.

Chapter 6 describes how we should think about choosing a developmental target.

Chapter 7 begins at a place familiar to all of us. In it, we describe how people go about learning any skill, including those skills having to do with leadership.

Chapter 8 explains a key step in becoming a better leader. This chapter describes the value of feedback and its role in helping leaders to develop. Feedback becomes especially valuable after someone begins functioning as a leader.

Chapter 9 describes action learning, or how to integrate daily on-the-job activities into your leadership development and elevate your strengths. If a great deal of valuable skill is learned on the job, then how do we become more deliberate and intentional in our integration of that with our development?

Chapter 10 focuses on how we can make this all more sustainable and how we truly lock into place many of these developmental activities so that they successfully expand the strengths we have selected.

Where to Start

Targeting Strengths to Develop

Should You Ever Work on a Weakness?

We are greatly amused at the consultants and writers who criticize those who focus on strengths. One of their most frequent arguments is that there are times when weaknesses need to be addressed. That idea seems so self-evident that it should go without saying. Does the person with a hand being burned on a hot plate need to ask if he should take his hand off? We would not think so.

But we thought we'd better be sure to say it now, and we will say it often. Are there times when you should work on a weakness? The answer is yes, absolutely. There are situations where you should temporarily set aside a strengths focus to correct a significant weakness. We will go into even greater detail in Chapter 12, but in the meantime, here are the questions we think leaders should ask themselves to determine whether a weakness is serious enough to warrant it being their initial development focus:

· Have I received feedback from any source that suggests that there is a harmful behavior or some habit that is holding me back in my job performance or career? This information could come from 360-degree feedback, performance reviews, or casual conversations with peers. (More frequently it will come from a spouse or significant other. One slightly amusing experience often occurs in feedback sessions with executives. In these sessions, they often will receive their 360-degree feedback report, or they will have the opportunity to receive some constructive [redirecting] feedback from us or others. After receiving the feedback, there will be a momentary pause, and then they will often say, "My [wife, husband, significant other] has been telling me that for years. Maybe I should have listened.")

CASE STUDY

One of the authors was coaching a senior executive who had received extremely harsh feedback from his boss, peers, and direct reports. It is very unusual for a person to receive such severe criticism, but in this case, he was absolutely slammed by all his rater categories. They saw him as focusing solely on results and regularly demonstrating behaviors that were demotivating to his peers, direct reports, and anyone else with whom he came in contact.

They described him as critical, demanding, unconcerned with facts and circumstances, and totally calloused toward people. The executive spent the first 90 minutes of the coaching session pretending complete surprise and shock, which then rapidly turned to anger with the feedback. He acted surprised, dismissive, and defiant and claimed everything must have been a mistake. He suggested there was probably an error made in the processing of the 360.

When he realized that was virtually not possible, he shifted to accusing his subordinates of being nonperforming idlers who deserved being treated the way he treated them. After 1½ hours of patient review and probing of his 360 results, he finally broke down and somewhat tearfully admitted to his coach that "not only is this completely accurate here at work; it's the exact same problem I have with my teenage sons at home. Please help me."

- Am I aware of anything negative about my leadership behavior that might stand out and overshadow my good qualities? Are there some damaging traits that have become characteristic of me to others that may be negatively defining me and my "personal brand"? Are there any such behaviors that could often be "top of mind" to those with whom I work?

Earlier we presented data showing that exceptional leaders possess three to five profound strengths. We need to add, however, that even with those strengths, leaders will have trouble being effective if they're really bad at anything. Our data show that for a leader with no profound strengths having just one very negative competency impacts a leader's overall perceived effectiveness by 15 percentile points. That's why we insert this caveat. If you possess a negative behavior that is detracting from your performance, then fix it. Fix it first. Fix it now. You are not alone. Recall that 28 percent of those we surveyed have scores that signal a potential fatal flaw.

The Payoffs from Strengths

In our research on the impact of strengths and fatal flaws, one thing that becomes very clear is the impact of having even one *profound strength* (meaning a competency that is perceived by others to be at the 90th percentile or higher). Leaders with no strengths who were able to develop just one profound strength moved their overall effectiveness rating as a leader from the 34th percentile to the 64th percentile. Consider the magnitude of this jump. This person would move from roughly the bottom third of the distribution of leaders to nearly the top third by simply executing one competency very well. As we have previously mentioned, fatal flaws also have a devastating negative impact. On average, leaders with one or more fatal flaws are rated at the 17th percentile.

The Importance of Setting Priorities

As we discuss leadership development with groups of executives, we often ask, "How many of you here are very busy in your lives and don't have a lot of spare time or energy?" Every hand goes up. We then ask, "Are any of you looking for a lot of extra projects to take on in addition to your existing workload and home responsibilities?" No hands go up. Everyone is busy and a bit overwhelmed. The thought of working to improve in three to five competencies seems impossible. Our goal in helping leaders develop is to give them a process to identify one competency to take on for improvement. From our experience, we know that if leaders will identify one critical competency and work hard to improve that competency, there will be a significant overall improvement in their leadership capability. In this chapter, we will describe a process that will help people identify the one competency that is the best one for them to develop.

The Importance of Knowing Where You Are

In the days before global positioning satellites and handheld devices that can now tell users their precise locations, military units operating in unfamiliar terrain faced a serious and millennia-old question: "Where the heck am I?" For a variety of military reasons, knowing one's precise location was critical. Needing to connect with other military units in coordinated attacks or defenses, being able to call for and direct reinforcements to your position, and even being able to successfully find your way back to friendly lines all depended on your knowing your current location.

Until recently, a standard training program for young army officers was to air-drop them into an unknown location—typically in the middle of a faraway forest or swamp—armed with only a map and a compass. The initial assignment was to use the map, compass, and visual observation to identify your drop-off location. Once determined, the next assignment was to quickly find your way to an assigned rendezvous point (of course, for motivation, the young officers typically hadn't eaten for hours and knew hot food was waiting at the destination).

The obvious beginning point of this training was to identify your starting location. What was the terrain like? What prominent features, like mountains, saddles, or ridgelines, stood out? Were there any observable rivers, lakes, or other water features? Together with compass and map, you could use these real-time observations to answer the question "Where the heck am I?" An accurate assessment of your current location was a vital first step. If you couldn't determine where you were, it would be very difficult to chart a path to your desired destination.

This is a useful analogy for all those interested in building their strengths. Without knowing your starting point, putting together a plan to get to your desired destination is impossible. Fortunately, there are several readily available instruments to help you identify your initial strengths. Many readers will be familiar with the book *Now Discover Your Strengths* by Marcus Buckingham and the instrument known as Strengthfinder that his former organization, the Gallup

Corporation, markets. While Strengthfinder is more specifically targeted to nonmanagerial or frontline individuals, it can be used across a wide variety of disciplines. Another instrument is known as VIA and is offered by the VIA Institute on Character. (The institute can be reached at info@VIAcharacter.org.) VIA consists of a rather lengthy questionnaire of 240 questions, and it enables an individual to take an in-depth look at his or her strengths. Both these instruments are self-administered and rely on the ability of a participant to combine being introspective and self-aware.

Possibly because of our extensive experience with a 360-degree feedback instrument, we lean strongly toward the use of a more objective analysis that goes beyond self-perceptions. We greatly value the perceptions of others if the data are possible to collect.

We frequently hear someone say, "Well, I know my strengths and weaknesses." The fact of the matter is that very few people have an accurate perception of either their strengths or their weaknesses. This is why we often comically read such facts as "80 percent of American drivers consider themselves above average" and "65 percent of people surveyed believe they are better than average looking in appearance." Indeed, our research shows that self-perceptions tend to be only half as reliable as those from either peers or direct reports, assuming that you use the total score from a 360-degree feedback instrument as the yardstick.

Figure 6.1 illustrates the ability of individual raters in each rater group to predict the overall leadership effectiveness score of the person being evaluated. This score is the average of all items assessing the effectiveness of a leader. The metric we are showing on the chart is a statistic called *r squared*. This is a measure of the amount of variance predicted by a statistical model.

It is interesting that managers in general are the most accurate predictors and that self-scores are only about half as accurate as that of any other rater group. We simply don't know our strengths or weaknesses as well as we would like to think we do.

Figure 6.1 Ability of Individuals in Each Rater Group
to Predict Overall Leadership Effectiveness

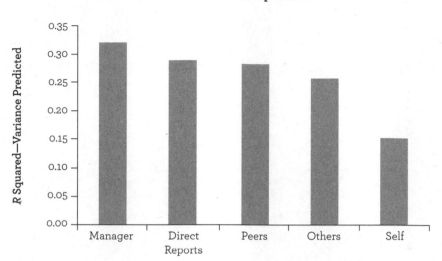

Why We Misperceive Our Strengths and Weaknesses

As we look at data from more than 27,000 leaders, it is interesting to see the trends of how people rate themselves versus how others rate them. Notice in Figure 6.2 that the worst leaders (those at the 1st through the 9th percentile) significantly overrate their ability. The best leaders (those at the 90th through the 100th percentile) significantly underrate their ability. This phenomenon has been noted by other researchers, such as Dunning and Kruger in their report, "Unskilled and Unaware of It: How Difficulties in Recognizing One's Own Incompetence Lead to Inflated Self-Assessments." These researchers basically found that people with poor skills consistently overrated their ability.

Figure 6.2 "Self" Versus "Others'" Perceptions of Our Effectiveness

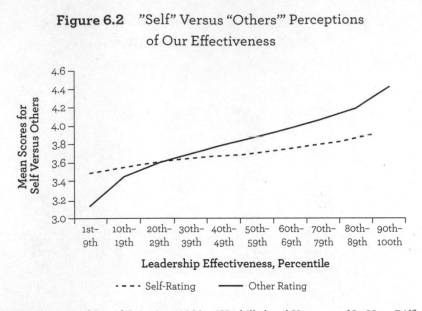

Justin Kruger and David Dunning (1999). "Unskilled and Unaware of It: How Difficulties in Recognizing One's Own Incompetence Lead to Inflated Self-Assessments," *Journal of Personality and Social Psychology* 77 (6): 1121–1134. doi:10.1037/ 0022-3514.77.6.1121. PMID 10626367

Everyone Has Strengths in Embryo

While it is relatively easy to identify competency areas in which a leader is considered proficient, the more difficult challenge is to identify those competencies that could and should be developed into a profound strength. Obviously the average leader will not have many of those. Only about one-third of leaders have one or more strengths at the 90th percentile, so don't be dismayed if you do not. These are developed by conscientious practice and effort.

Nearly every leader has a group of competencies that are average or above average. These are the prime candidates for development into a strength. Choose to view these as your strengths in embryo.

Choosing What to Make into a Strength

We propose a model with three important filters for identifying a behavior that could be expanded into a strength. We label this the *CPO model*, where C stands for "competence," P for "passion," and O for "organization need." The basic premise of the CPO model is to consider each of its three key filters when selecting a competency for development into a strength:

1. *Competence.* The first consideration is to measure the level of competence. Is this competency a strength in embryo? What are your current inclinations and abilities? What are you already reasonably effective at doing?

   For example, John is known to be a good problem solver. People come to him when they have a thorny problem they are wrestling with. He is also highly regarded as a collaborative team player. People find it easy to work with John, and he brings energy to the groups in which he works. John's 360-degree feedback scores on these competencies show both problem solving and collaboration to be just below the 75th percentile.

   John could select either of these competencies as ones to be developed into noteworthy strengths. He began with a head start. These have come relatively easy to him. We'd call these "strengths in embryo."

2. *Passion.* What charges your batteries? It is one thing to be reasonably effective at some leadership competency that is compatible with what the organization needs, but it takes on a different cast if it is something for which you have little or no enthusiasm. Frankly, there are elements to most leadership roles that involve activities that the organization needs to have done and that you do acceptably, but they make you feel like you are drinking mud.

For many of us, this would be something like completing an expense report. Over the years, most of us have become reasonably adept at doing that. The organization needs it for many purposes, including meeting internal control requirements and satisfying the IRS. But there are few who really find this very exciting. Preparing the annual budget is another activity that often falls in the same category. But it is also important to remember that not everybody feels the same way about an activity. For some people, preparing a communication plan designed to get all the recently agreed-upon plans disseminated to everyone in the division would be huge drudgery. Yet for others, it could be the pinnacle of fun and a highly rewarding project.

As another example, many parents insist that their children learn to play a musical instrument. Those with more than one child have undoubtedly noticed the differing reactions to these lessons. Some children attend their lessons willingly, practice for hours without undue drama, and become reasonably good at, say, the piano. A granddaughter of one of the authors said, after a year of lessons, "I want to be really good!" Her mother found a renowned teacher at a local university, and the granddaughter went on to win awards in international competitions. She willingly practiced three to four hours per day.

On the other hand, not only do some children *not* show interest, but they balk at taking lessons and resist practicing for even a half hour each day. The difference in resulting skill levels and proficiency between these children—the passionate versus the dispassionate—does not appear to be the result of any inborn talent, but much more the passion felt toward the process of learning to play.

As we coach leaders, helping them to improve, we have seen some make a major discovery in identifying areas of passion.

The discovery helps them focus their development in areas that charge their batteries—ones that are not just important and rewarding to their organizations, but also important and rewarding to them personally.

3. *Organization need.* What does your organization need from you right now in your current position? Regardless of what you are currently effective at doing, the value of developing strengths that will enhance your career and help you become a more competent leader is obviously specific to the organization in which you work and the current position you hold. A sales manager clearly requires widely different skills from those of the person in charge of the audit department. The operations manager requires different skills from those of the head of research and development. The selection of a quality to develop should always factor in the organization, your assignment, and what they need from you.

Even within the same organization, the competencies needed by similar functional leaders may vary significantly. For example, different business strategies or models among different sales teams in the same business unit can drive very different competency needs for their leaders. One sales team may be focused on direct sales to customers, and another team in the same group sells through channel partners. Those different sales teams may require different critical competencies from the two different sales managers leading them.

The ideal situation occurs when these three CPO elements come together. It is perfect when the individual can be working on a competency that he or she is already reasonably good at doing, when that competency is something that the organization highly values, and when the individual has an intense interest in and passion for building the competency.

CASE STUDY

One of the authors was coaching an executive in a large high-technology firm. The executive was newly promoted into a senior position responsible for a significant piece of the organization. Feedback from her peers, manager, and direct reports praised her excellent interpersonal skills and her focus on getting results. And each noted that in her new role, she would benefit from an ability to be more strategic in her thinking about the business. As she and the coach talked about this strategic thinking competence she needed to develop, it was clear that this was a developmental opportunity that fit exactly into the CPO pattern. She was perceived as being above average, but not outstanding, in doing this. The organization very much needed this from her in her new role, and she was extremely interested in getting better at doing it.

As luck would have it, she was about to embark on an international trip along with several other company executives. On this trip, they would meet with government officials in China, India, and other Asia-Pacific countries. She would also be meeting with senior executives from important customers in these countries. And she would be traveling in the same group with two leaders in the firm who were recognized as being extremely astute in strategic thinking and planning. In fact, one had held a corporate strategic planning staff role before his current assignment. She and her coach planned on how she could use this opportunity to expand her thinking about her industry, identifying the major forces within it, the longer-term future for her division, key customers' hot buttons and concerns, and ways to use this opportunity to discuss her division's long-term plans with her colleagues who were recognized for doing that well.

In subsequent conversations with this executive, it was clear that she used this experience as a crash course in strategic thinking. Her colleagues and boss saw her passion and her dedicated response to feedback that had been constructively offered to her.

Behaviors That Make a Difference

One of the important conclusions from our initial research was that amid the hundreds of traits and abilities that could be measured, some were extremely important, and others made little or no difference on perceived leadership effectiveness. At one end of the spectrum is the quality of *punctuality for business meetings*. We discovered that leaders who were extremely effective were on time for business meetings, but we found that an equal number of quite ineffective executives were also on time for meetings. Punctuality for meetings and appointments was simply not a differentiating competency. Focusing effort, therefore, on improving punctuality would not make one whit of difference on how the individual would be perceived as a leader.

There were, however, some behaviors that showed substantial differences between the best and worst leaders. We examined multiple data sets and tested approximately 2,000 different behaviors. After looking at results from over 20,000 leaders based on assessments from over 200,000 respondents, we determined that there was a very consistent set of competencies that separated the best from the worst leaders. As we have tested and utilized these competencies over the last few years, we have found that improvement activities on these behaviors are more noticeable and create substantially greater impact. As noted earlier in the book, we call these behaviors the 16 differentiating competencies. Table 6.1 shows the 16 behaviors clustered into five different competency areas.

Table 6.1   The 16 Differentiating Competencies

Focus on Results	Leading Change	Character	Interpersonal Skills	Personal Capability
Drives for results	Develops strategic perspective	Displays integrity and honesty	Communicates powerfully and prolifically	Has technical/ professional expertise
Establishes stretch goals	Champions change		Inspires and motivates others to high performance	Solves problems and analyzes issues
Takes initiative	Connects the group to the outside world		Builds relationships	Innovates
			Develops others	Practices self-development
			Engages in collaboration and teamwork	

So a great filter to help determine which competency a leader might select to develop would be to check any competency being considered against the list of the 16 differentiating ones. Working on one of these differentiating competencies has been shown by our research to have a substantially greater impact than working on others.

We did further analysis using our global database to understand which of the 16 differentiating competencies were, in fact, the most differentiating. The following 5 competencies were at the top of the list (and are listed in rank order):

1. Inspires and motivates others to high performance

2. Communicates powerfully and prolifically

3. Establishes stretch goals

4. Develops strategic perspective

5. Solves problems and analyzes issues

Looking more closely at *inspires and motivates others,* we found that in addition to being the most differentiating, it was also the most highly correlated with high levels of employee engagement. Direct reports deemed it to be the most important and desirable trait they wanted in their leader.

When selecting a competency to further develop, this additional list of the 5 competencies that were the *most* differentiating could be helpful. It could be used as a further filter when deciding between 2 or more of the 16 differentiating competencies being considered.

Our conclusion is simple. When choosing a competency to build into a strength, choose one that makes a whopping difference.

Conclusions

The selection of which strengths to develop is obviously an important decision. We have first noted that there are times when working on a weakness is precisely the correct thing to do. For most leaders, however, our research shows that working on a strength is the better path to follow. How to choose that strength is not an exact science. It involves combining several factors, and in the CPO model we have noted three that seem particularly important. First, identify a competency in which you're already reasonably proficient and can show clear improvement. Do not choose something already at the 90th percentile, because there is little room for progress. Second, identify those traits and behaviors for which you have some passion. Selecting a competency that you'd enjoy developing further will help you stay focused and interested in that effort. Third, consider what the organization needs from you. Further developing a competency important to your current assignment can mean an immediate increase in your job effectiveness.

Transitioning from Poor Performance to Good

A Linear Plan for Enhancing Your Skills

Modeling: The Beginning of Developing Any Skill or Ability

Let's start with the most basic of skills. In Chapter 3 we introduced the process that we all went through in learning to dress ourselves or eat meals using a knife and fork. How did we learn these skills? We observed others. Children mimic their parents. The child watches carefully as the parent shows how to tie shoelaces into a bow, and then the child imitates and practices those actions. Aspiring physicians acquire their skills as they first watch experienced surgeons perform an operation and then assist in the procedure. We learned most of our skills by watching others perform them. We then selected those actions that seemed feasible and comfortable for us to duplicate.

The same principle holds true for the acquisition of any leadership skill. Young employees in an organization watch how the boss conducts a meeting. They watch how the boss delegates an assignment. They watch how the boss responds to questions regarding the organization or replies to a customer about the firm's products. This obviously is more readily applied to the overt, behavioral side of leadership and management in contrast to the cerebral activities of the executive.

Others learn, however, when leaders share their thought processes, assumptions, and experience. That is one of the great virtues of having senior executives come in to teach in leadership development programs. That exposure to senior executives has become a cornerstone of many companies' leadership development efforts. It is also one of the great benefits of having a young executive work as an assistant to a senior leader. The apprentice leader learns from hearing the senior leader discuss the thought processes that led to specific decisions. A *Harvard Business Review* blog in 2012 by Jack Zenger and Joe Folkman noted research from data collected in 2011 comparing men versus women in terms of their leadership effectiveness. The data came from Zenger Folkman clients. The study showed that women were significantly more effective on 12 of 16 competencies. Not surprisingly, this blog drew a large number of reactions. One of the themes from the reactions to the blog was women mentioning the importance of senior leaders as coaches and mentors during critical periods of their careers. Many noted that the mentors were male. The point of the study was not to prove that women are superior to men but rather to highlight that when people are highly motivated to achieve, to get developmental job assignments, and to receive coaching and mentoring, leadership skills can be developed.

The noted management expert and writer, Peter Drucker, often told the following story about the legendary corporate chieftain Alfred P. Sloan, Jr., head of General Motors in the 1920s:

At a meeting of one of GM's top committees, there had been a lengthy discussion about the wisdom of locating a new plant in a foreign country. A good deal of factual information about the intended plant and the new location had been presented. Every comment and question regarding the proposal from the entire committee had been warm and positive. Sloan said, "Gentleman, I take it we are all in complete agreement on the subject here." Heads nodded around the table.

"Then," Sloan continued, taking the group aback, "I propose we not approve this matter now, and that we postpone further discussion of it until our next meeting. We need to give ourselves time to develop disagreement and perhaps gain some understanding of what the decision is all about."

This was obviously a stunning lesson to all who attended on both the value and the necessity of substantive disagreement. Good decisions are more likely to occur when there is an open exploration of conflicting points of view. The lesson has also been passed on to countless other leaders who have heard the story told again and again.

This early process of learning skills happens quite casually and informally. Seldom is it scripted or planned in any detail. Some have estimated that as much as 70 percent of what we learn comes from such casual learning. That statistic has been oft-repeated in HR circles. The fact of the matter is that it came from a single event in which a facilitator of a management training session asked the roughly 30 participants to assess as best they could where they had learned their leadership skills. Was it from formal classroom training, was it from coaching, or was it from the daily routine events that occurred on the job? The participants replied, and on average they thought that their learning had come 70 percent from their job, 20 percent from coaching, and 10 percent from formal, classroom-type training. While the conclusion may be directionally correct, it was not the most rigorous of research endeavors.

As it turns out, we cannot find any definitive studies that would answer that question. However, we can all agree that informal and casual learning is a major source of knowledge and skill acquisition. Given that no one knows the exact answer, let's agree not to fret about the exact magnitude of it.

Formal Development

Added to this is the role of formal development that the organization or some outside source provides. In some skill areas, such as learning how to use various software applications for the computer, formal classes can provide extremely helpful information and jump-start a person's progress. Formal development can be separated into two categories, individual skill development and process skill development.

Individual Skill Development

New supervisors are often given the opportunity to acquire the people management skills demanded of good supervision. Most organizations use a behavior modeling technology in which video clips are shown with managers handling difficult situations well. The course content explains the key action steps that were being followed. The bulk of the learning process involves participants practicing and rehearsing these skills with one another and giving feedback to one another.

A popular leadership skill teaches participants how to make more effective presentations to groups. Increasingly, organizations provide formal development to their leaders on the art of coaching and selection interviewing.

Process Skill Development

A good example of process skill development is sales training. It extends over numerous interactions and links multiple skills (making cold calls, discovering needs, ensuring understanding, dealing with objections, questioning, strategizing, negotiating, and closing). Here, an ideal process framework or concept is presented, the process is broken down into discrete steps, applications of (or case studies using) the process are analyzed, and the process steps may even be practiced.

There has been some debate about the relative value and contribution of such formal training in comparison to merely learning on the job. While it is clear that a great deal is learned in a casual and informal way, such formal training can be of enormous benefit, especially when compared with the amount of time being spent.

Coaching

Another extremely important source of development comes from the formal and informal coaching received from one's boss, peers, or external coach. Surveys show that it is extremely rare that individuals believe they receive enough coaching from their bosses, let alone too much. Nearly everyone relishes the opportunity to receive more coaching. Organizations are aggressively pursuing the development of their leaders into better coaches.

CASE STUDY

For a global phone call with coaches and facilitators from around the world who are affiliated with our firm, we had

(continues)

(continued)

invited a guest to make a presentation. She is the human resource executive from one of the largest banks in the United States who is in charge of the bank's overall coaching efforts. In the course of her remarks, she made a rather startling comment to the group. She said that senior management of the bank had set the target for their mid-level managers to spend approximately two-thirds of their time coaching their subordinates. You could almost hear the gasps of surprise. Bank executives had obviously made the determination that their future success hinged on the development of people at lower levels and that managers should ideally be spending far more time in this activity.

Coaching and Generational Differences

We recently conducted an analysis of leaders from different generations that we believe sheds some light on this subject. We looked at data from the classic four generations:

Generation	Born between
1. Traditionalists (or silents)	1925 and 1945
2. Baby boomers	1946 and 1954
3. Gen X	1955 and 1976
4. Gen Y	1977 and 1998

As this book is being written, the baby boomers are currently reaching traditional retirement age. In the United States, they number more than 25 million. In sheer size, this is a much larger group than Gen X. Their departure will leave a huge void. Results from analyzing our data suggest that the most significant difference between the boomers and the Gen Y group is in the area of technical and professional expertise. Our data show that boomers are perceived as being much more technically and professional expert, some 11 percentile points higher than their Gen Y counterparts.

It becomes easy to understand why the bank in our case study, referred to earlier, places such high emphasis on increased coaching. They foresee that there will be a huge drain of technical knowledge. This expertise must somehow be passed on. The other driving force is the huge expressed need on the part of the Gen Y group to learn how to be better leaders. One-on-one coaching from senior leaders is a powerful way to learn these skills, probably the best way. This combination of passing on technical knowledge and acquiring greater leadership perspective and skills is, in our opinion, driving the surge in coaching in today's organizations.

One challenge with coaching is that it demands from those who practice it one of the more difficult activities that humans ever experience. It requires unlearning old habits. It also requires completely changing a mindset. Say the word *coaching*, and the average person instantly thinks of what he or she experienced in junior high school, high school, or college sports. One can scarcely imagine any activity where there is a higher level of flat-out autocratic leadership being practiced. The junior high and high school coach decides who will play, where they will play, when they will play, and what the game strategy will be—and often calls the specific plays during the game. This is the complete antithesis of good coaching in a business context.

The other major perception that exists about coaching is that coaching is basically giving advice. In the book *The Extraordinary Coach*,[1] the authors offer this definition of coaching: "Interactions that help the individual being coached to expand awareness, discover superior solutions, and make and implement better decisions." Notice the absence in this definition of giving advice or telling people what they should do.

Indeed, we have found that the most frequent outcomes of training people to be better coaches are that they resolve to:

- Talk less, not more than 20 percent of the conversation
- Ask more questions
- Listen more intently
- Refrain from giving advice
- Plan the interview more thoroughly

Just last year one of the authors was in Mexico with a group of 20 executives conducting a training program to increase coaching effectiveness. The author asked the question, "How many of you have ever had a discussion with your manager where he or she really took the time to understand your perspective and point of view before offering you advice?" The author was looking for a few volunteers to describe what that experience was like and the impact that it had on them. As the author looked over the group, no hands went up. The question was repeated and still no hands. Not one executive there had ever been given the chance to express concerns or perspectives before being given advice. Real coaching is rare, but when the skill is mastered, it can have a substantial impact on the learning of others.

Practice

Much has been written in recent years about the role of practice in acquiring a skill. While there has never been much doubt about the need for practice in acquiring a skill, more recent research has escalated the role of practice to an even higher level.

There has long been the adage "Practice makes perfect." That has been refined by those who point out that not all practice leads to perfection. Indeed, you can be practicing the wrong thing, or you can be practicing doing the right thing in the wrong way. The more correct adage would say, "Perfect practice makes perfect."

Add to that another useful insight. There's practice, and there's deliberate practice. Merely going out to hit a bucket of golf balls doesn't necessarily improve someone's golf game in any measurable way. But creating a circle 15 feet in diameter with chalk or white tape on the grass, standing back 50 yards, and then proceeding to hit a bucket of balls until you are able to place 80 percent in the circle will make a difference in your game. Then, moving back a few yards and using a different iron and again hitting a bucket of balls until you can land 80 percent in the circle constitutes deliberate practice. Such practice truly makes a difference.

The capstone of research on practice has come from professors at the Florida State University, as they studied the phenomenon of expert performance. There has been a long-held belief that child prodigies were born with an unusual portion of talent, and that accounted for their remarkable performance. Dr. Anders Ericsson and his colleagues have convincingly shown that expert performance begins in childhood with extensive, deliberate practice under the tutelage of a concerned adult, and the level of performance achieved is the direct result of the number of hours spent in practice, extending over a period of 10 years or more. In short, practice is an extremely key element in the acquisition of any complex skill.

Linear Development Works for Beginners and Those Correcting Weaknesses

Each of the sections in this chapter (modeling, formal development, coaching, and practice) represents a form of training that we have called linear development. The strength of this approach is that it is highly efficient and is perfectly adapted to someone learning a new skill. That is readily seen from the examples we've provided. It also works when someone is coming from a point of deficiency and seeking to move upward. There is an inherent logic about what is being recommended. Linear development activities have a strong "face validity."

For example, one of the differentiating competencies is *develops others*. Following are some linear activities that a manager could initiate to build this competency:

- Encouraging the organization to provide formal training
- Identifying training programs that will improve performance and skills
- Delegating tasks that require people to stretch and acquire new skills and knowledge
- Inviting junior employees to work with him on projects
- Reviewing and refining each individual's career plans and development
- Building the visibility and credibility of junior colleagues by touting their accomplishments to others in the organization
- Scheduling regular coaching sessions with the individual

It should be obvious that these would all be appropriate suggestions for a new manager or for one with several years under her belt but who had not fully developed her people.

Implications and Applications

As we find leaders with exceptional skills and ask them how they developed these important capabilities, often we hear a very similar story. The story starts with them being given a new job assignment. The new assignment is very different from anything they had done before and required them to use skills they had never developed previously. They often admit that at first their efforts to perform these skills were not very good, but the team was patient with them, and their manager gave them some coaching assistance. Over time, the skills were developed and improved. The leaders moved from being unskilled to skilled and eventually to becoming experts.

Conclusion

The beginning stages of acquiring a skill are well known to all of us. We have used them since the beginning of our lives. They have enabled us to learn skills in virtually every dimension of what we do, including the skills to manage and lead inside an organization. The processes used are logical and obvious.

CHAPTER 8

The Role of Feedback in Developing Leadership Strengths

A Surefire Medicine

Improving Performance

Several HR professionals were asked, "What is the most effective learning or teaching method ever devised?" On most topics in the human resources arena, there are invariably sharp differences of opinion. Not many subjects come close to being cut and dried. But this was one of those rare topics on which a group of professionals agreed. Their unhesitating choice was the flight simulator. Why?

This remarkable equipment and software re-creates real situations that a pilot might encounter. These range from severe weather patterns and electrical storms to equipment malfunction and an inadvertent incursion by one plane into another's flight path. The beauty of the flight simulator is that pilots can practice responding to all these situations without the slightest danger to any human lives. While not as important as saving human life, the flight simulator also minimizes loss and damage to expensive airplanes. Potentially dangerous events can be repeated until the proper action becomes second nature to the pilot.

The superiority of the flight simulator as a teaching device is that as the pilot practices, there is immediate feedback that tells the pilot if the actions taken were right or wrong, safe or dangerous. The feedback comes instantly from multiple instruments and software outputs. The feedback is direct and unfiltered. Further, it isn't watered down because some other human is worried about hurting the pilot's feelings.

The basic purpose of this feedback could be described as "closing the loop," to let another person who is performing some task or function know of the outcomes from his or her actions. The underlying objective is to be helpful and to give people information that will enable them to improve their performance the next time around.

The Motivating Effect of Feedback

The *New York Times* ran a fascinating story on the impact of feedback on physical performance. This experiment was conducted by Kevin Thompson, the head of sport and exercise science at the Northumbrian University in England. The experiment had to do with bicyclists who thought they had ridden as fast as they possibly could. In this experiment, he did something that scientists do not like to do, which is to trick their subjects. But the experiment demanded that.

The design of this research had cyclists put on stationary bicycles and asked to pedal as vigorously as they could for the time that would cover roughly a 2.5 mile distance. They repeated this several times in order to establish a benchmark that defined their peak effort. The trickery came after that.

As reported in the *New York Times* of September 19, 2011:

Each rider was shown two avatars. One was himself, moving along a virtual course at the rate he was actually pedaling the stationary bicycle at the current time. The other figure was moving at the pace of the cyclist's best effort—or so the cyclists were told.

In fact, the second avatar was programmed to ride faster than the cyclist ever had—using 2 percent more power, which translates into a 1 percent increase in speed. Told to race against what they thought was their own best time, the cyclists ended up matching their avatars on their virtual rides, going significantly faster than they ever had gone before.

In the mind of many of us, a 2 percent increase in power might seem rather inconsequential, but in the elite sport of competitive cycling, a 1 percent change in speed makes the difference between being in front of the pack and wearing a yellow shirt versus bringing up the rear. The improvements shown in this experiment represented "a true change in performance" according to Thompson.

Another sports psychologist, Timothy Noakes, also a professor of exercise and sports science at the University of Cape Town in South Africa, refers to the brain as the central governor, because it is the force that sets the pace and determines the level of effort, which ultimately determines the final performance of the athlete.

In the past those who studied physical performance were interested primarily in the hearts, muscles, and lungs of the athletes. The assumption was that these organs have an outer limit of performance. They were believed by many to be the gaiting factor. However, Roger Bannister, the man who originally broke the 4-minute-mile barrier, spoke on behalf of countless athletes when he said, "It is the brain, not the heart or lungs, that is the critical organ. It's the brain."

A key competency of any successful leader, then, is the ability to continually gather, accept, and respond to feedback. Still, the collection of feedback, while helpful, is not enough. Just hearing feedback does not necessarily mean that individuals will accept that feedback and adjust their behavior. In this chapter, we will discuss the factors that help people to accept and move forward on their feedback.

Asking for Feedback

Asking for and receiving feedback is a key skill for every leader. Data collected from thousands of respondents on the coaching behavior of their boss confirm that asking for feedback is the behavior on which these leaders received the lowest single score. Fortunately, the managers who were being evaluated agreed with the feedback they received. Leaders are not prone to ask for feedback from anyone, not their bosses, nor their peers, nor their subordinates.

This is obviously unfortunate, because by asking for feedback, the leaders would be acting as good role models for subordinates. Their behavior should encourage their subordinates to seek feedback from them. And, further, the leaders could be excellent examples of how to respond nondefensively to honest feedback.

Generational Differences in Asking for Feedback

One of the problems with leaders asking for feedback is that the older people become, the less frequently they ask for feedback. Figure 8.1 shows age by 5-year increments. The results displayed are percentile scores of 360 ratings on the item *actively looks for opportunities to get feedback to improve him/herself*. The data for this study come from 4,674 leaders, and the percentiles are calculated by comparing these leaders with those in our global normative database. Note that people 25 or younger score at the 71st percentile in looking for feedback.

Figure 8.1   Looks for Opportunities to Get Feedback, by Age

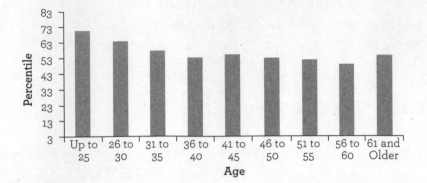

That number steadily declines down to the 49th percentile for people between 56 and 60. It is encouraging that those 61 and older begin to improve on this item.

Cutting the same data by level in the organization, we also discovered that executives and senior managers were rated significantly lower in their desire to look for opportunities to get feedback than individual contributors and supervisors. Figure 8.2 shows the results.

Why do these numbers generally decline with age and increased level in the organization? One explanation could be that these older and more senior leaders believe that because they have been promoted to senior positions, they are especially capable and therefore less in need of feedback. "I must be really good, or I wouldn't be where I am." Or is it because they know that junior people in the organization are reluctant to give feedback to senior people? Therefore, why bother trying? They will just tell you what they think you want to hear. Still another possibility is that senior leaders are beset by the twin demons of arrogance and complacency. Do they come to believe that "I am what I am, and I'm too old to change"? Is getting feedback, therefore, a waste of time? We believe these are a few of the assumptions that get them into trouble. The senior leaders are obviously doing many things right, but asking for feedback appears to be an area in which they could as a group improve.

Figure 8.2 Looks for Opportunities to Get Feedback, by Level in the Organization

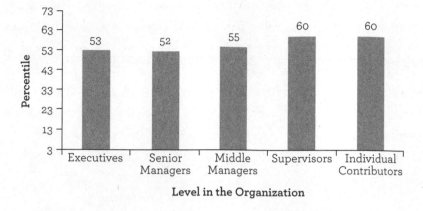

When we look at the willingness of a leader to ask others for feedback, we find that there is an excellent correlation to overall leadership effectiveness. You can see in Figure 8.3 that leaders who are at the bottom 10 percent in their willingness to ask for feedback are only at the 17th percentile in terms of overall leadership effectiveness, while those at the top 10 percent are at the 83rd percentile.

Figure 8.3 Seeking Feedback

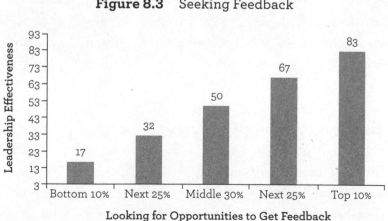

Who is the best person to determine what makes you happy? You. Who is the best person to determine what foods you like? You. Who is the best person to determine your effectiveness at dealing with others? You? Actually no—it's other people. While people as individuals may or may not be correct in their opinions, the only way to get an accurate read of how you are doing as a leader is through the collective eyes of those you lead. The more distant we become from the realities of others, the more distorted our views become of how we are really doing. Bottom line, a leader's ability to lead is highly determined by the reactions of others to that leader. Self-perceptions make little difference.

Accepting Feedback

People can only benefit from feedback if they believe and accept the feedback they've been given. The classic example is the alcoholic whose spouse says, "You have a drinking problem." The alcoholic says, "No, it's not really that bad. I don't have a problem." Then the employer notices the drinking problem. The alcoholic replies again, "It's not a problem." Eventually this person gets divorced and is fired by his or her employer. The person ends up as a derelict on the street. One morning, the individual wakes up sleeping in a cardboard box in a doorway and finally says, "I think I have a problem." That moment is when change can start. It happens when the person accepts the feedback and realizes the need to change.

Skills of Accepting Feedback

Accepting feedback is a function of four broad sets of skills. *First and most fundamental is the ability to be humble and reflective.* Humility comes when people start to understand that it is the reactions of others that really matter in terms of their leadership effectiveness. Their effectiveness as a leader is determined by others. Leadership is all about the ability to influence others, and so it is those others who have all the data and the insights. Your opinion makes little difference. The opinions of others make a huge difference. This attitude of focusing on the opinions of others is difficult for some leaders because some don't really care much about the opinions of those they lead. While some people would subscribe to the belief that everyone ought to respect others' opinions, the reality is that we care about some opinions much more than others. One very effective way to help leaders gain humility is to have them ask for feedback from people whom they greatly respect. Getting feedback from people who are critical to your future success will automatically cause you to be concerned about the feedback. What many people quickly discover when they accept feedback from respected others is that this feedback is essentially the same as the feedback they have received from those whom they respected to a lesser degree.

The second factor is personal honesty and integrity. People who are more honest and straightforward with others tend to be honest and straightforward with themselves. People who shade the truth, even slightly with others, will have the same tendency to shade the truth to themselves. People who deceive others will deceive themselves. Many people are capable of lying to themselves and then over time believing their own lies.

The path to improvement starts with being honest, direct, and straightforward with others. Many who read this description will think of people who are crooks as examples of the dishonest. But there is abundant dishonesty from people who are trying to protect others or insulate them from the harsh realities of the world. Some managers, rather than being straightforward and honest with direct reports about where they stand, tell them what they want to hear. That dishonesty is as much a lie as dishonesty for personal gain. Being absolutely honest with ourselves is a key skill that will build both success as a leader and success in life. Too many people are self-deceived. Too many people assume either greatness or complete failure when the reality is different.

This tendency is confirmed by Figure 8.4, which compares the level of honesty and integrity that a person possesses, as perceived by their boss, their peers, and their direct reports. The higher the level of perceived honesty and integrity, the higher the level of openness to receiving feedback from those about you.

The third factor is engaging in the development of others. Our research indicated that those who were better at accepting feedback also tended to be more effective at developing others. Development is contagious. When people do it for others, some of it is bound to rub off. Having the perspective that others ought to improve and develop new skills makes it much more likely that they themselves will be open to feedback on what they can do to improve. One of the powerful tools to develop others is to provide them with useful feedback. That works best, however, when the leader has set the example by seeking feedback from the subordinate, welcoming any and all messages that would help the leader to be ever more effective.

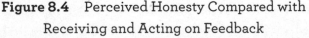

Figure 8.4   Perceived Honesty Compared with Receiving and Acting on Feedback

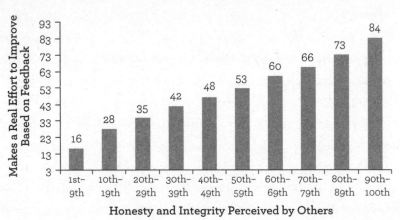

The final factor is taking action and initiative to move forward and respond to the feedback. Passive acceptance is a helpful start, but without action, nothing changes. Those who accept feedback and move forward start to respond with energy and enthusiasm about improving their performance. They provide others with a clear vision and goal about what they are going to change and how they will do it. Finally, after they start, they follow through on their commitment to execute the change.

360-Degree Feedback

One of our favorite feedback mechanisms is 360-degree feedback. Here's why we are such fans. First of all, we're not a slim minority. We estimate that approximately 85 percent of the Fortune 500 companies use 360-degree feedback as an integral part of their development process. Why? Bottom line, they have found that it works effectively. Leaders gain information they would otherwise never receive. They can get actionable assessments of how they're perceived in specific, meaningful leadership competency areas. These provide a clear picture of how they're performing and what impact they're having on the organization. That picture forms the basis for developing a plan to become more effective. By providing anonymity to peers, direct reports, and other potential raters, the leader is able to receive candid, open, honest feedback from those around her. For many this will be a first.

Critics of the 360-degree process have argued that it is a crutch. They argue that people should have the courage and the commitment to the organization to provide information to colleagues in a completely forthcoming manner. That should hold true for feedback to a subordinate, to a peer, or to the most senior people in the organization. When we hear that argument, we have to smile. Yes, that would be ideal. That's how the world should be. But let's get real. It isn't that way now, and we don't expect it to change any time soon.

More than 90 percent of organizations utilizing 360-degree feedback elect to use an external supplier for this. Clearly most of these organizations have the IT bandwidth to do something like this internally, but they have concluded that the confidentiality and anonymity offered by the external supplier is something of great value and that there are other higher priorities for their internal IT department. Chances are, the vendor's instrument they end up using is also much more sophisticated than one they would develop in-house and includes access to normative data from various other organizations and industries. Most organizations find this to be a classic example of where outsourcing makes sense. Creating, testing, running, and maintaining validated 360-degree survey systems are not seen as strategic or "core" competencies for most Fortune 500 companies. That is why they rely on external suppliers for whom this is their core competency and raison d'être.

We felt this topic to be of such prime importance that we have devoted Chapter 14 solely to the 360-degree surveys and what organizations should be looking for when they choose to use one. We are struck by the enormous differences in instruments, their simplicity, their ease of interpretation, and the science underlying them.

Coaching as an Additional Mechanism for Feedback

We wrote about coaching in the previous chapter. It is a way to learn a skill. It is also a way to fine-tune and improve a skill. There are many effective ways for feedback to be given to leaders. One of the most powerful vehicles is the use of coaches. These people can be external to the firm, or they can be internal. Many organizations are experimenting with the use of peer coaches. Coaching becomes, in essence, a giant mirror being held up to the individual. In this mirror, individuals can learn things about their behavior and its impact that they could learn in virtually no other way.

Most people have elected to comb their hair while looking in a mirror. It is hard to see whether the part in your hair is straight without that reflected image. Similarly, there are many aspects of our behavior that we simply cannot see without the help of some feedback in the form of a 360 or from a coach who is genuinely dedicated to a leader's development.

Feedback Can Be Fun

Why do people all over the world enjoy participating in games and sports? Why have games and sports been going on for not just centuries, but millennia? One of the theories is that they provide immediate feedback. The batter in a neighborhood game of softball knows immediately if he hits or misses the ball. If it is hit, it is clear whether it is in bounds or a foul ball. It's clear if it bobbles into the infield or sails over the fence for a home run. The tennis player learns immediately how the angle of the racket and the strength of the swing cause the ball to be returned too low and hit the net or if it is hit too high and too hard it goes out of bounds. Indeed, a good part of the joy and appeal of every sport is this immediate feedback. It also enables the player to make an infinite number of adjustments necessary to improve performance.

A final comment about feedback has to do with helping organizations to become feedback-rich environments in which information flows freely and is accepted and acted upon. It is obviously not enough to simply have feedback given if it is angrily rejected or dismissed because of the source. There is a Swedish proverb that says "With the eating comes the appetite." We have found that the more that feedback is shared in organizations, the more easily it is digested and acted upon. Attitudes about feedback in companies that have been doing 360-degree feedback for 25 years are extremely different from those doing it for the first time. We've found that within organizations that routinely provide feedback, there is a much higher degree of eagerness to get data. At the same time, there is a calm and ease about being able to dismiss the occasional outlier number or comment. By that, we mean the one person out of nine who rates a leader as needing improvement on an item, when all others perceived this as being a strength. With greater confidence and ease, the leader says, "All the rest were positive, and so I'm not overly concerned about this one outlier. It's good to know that someone sees me differently, but I'm not going to lose sleep over it."

Conclusion

The chapters in Part II of the book address ways by which people can build strengths. We can think of no activity, which if broadly practiced in an organization, will have more beneficial impact on building strengths in leaders than if they learn to readily give and receive feedback; but especially to freely ask for feedback from those around them.

First, let's acknowledge that there are enormous benefits when bosses provide feedback to colleagues. People want to know how they're doing. Most want to continually get better. Receiving feedback is a great way for that to happen.

Such feedback could be positive reinforcement exclusively, or it could be something like "Great presentation, Jim. Good information and really clear graphs of what's been happening. Next time, could I suggest that you give a few examples—tell some stories. That's what convinces this senior team as much as the data."

Or it could be more difficult feedback that is intended to correct behavior that detracts from performance.

"Greg, are you open to hearing some information about how people are reacting to some of your recent e-mails on cost containment?"

"Yeah, sure. What have you heard?"

"Well, people think you are focused on some inconsequential items, like delivery costs and packaging materials; and that you put the customer's interests way below saving a few pennies on the delivery of an order. Now, I know we need to keep some balance, but I've looked over your e-mails and listened to what others are feeling. I believe they are correct. You've put way too much emphasis on the small stuff."

That's direct feedback, and for most of us, it is the hardest to give. And let's face it, the great majority of managers shy away from giving feedback like this. Such messages are uncomfortable at best, and downright painful at worst. The arguments in favor of doing it are not only that it leads to better performance, but that it also greatly increases the level of employee engagement.

We have some new research that shows that there is an even better way to increase employee engagement. Surprisingly, the secret is for the manager to ask for feedback. The impact of asking for it is even more powerful than the impact of giving it. Here's what happens to the percentile scores on employee engagement:

- 29th percentile—manager neither asks for, nor gives feedback
- 34th percentile—manager doesn't ask, but gives feedback
- 48th percentile—manager asks to receive feedback, but doesn't give feedback
- 74th percentile—manager both asks for and gives feedback

Good things come from asking for feedback. Seeking the opinions of others has a host of benefits. It conveys your respect. It reduces barriers between the levels. Managers learn valuable information that comes in no other way. Empirically it reduces by 10 percent the number of employees who intend to leave.

Clearly the ideal is for managers to both give and get, but if you had to choose one or the other, our data suggests that it is better to receive than to give.

CHAPTER 9

Building Strengths at Work

Integrating On-the-Job Activities into Your Growth as a Leader

As we continue to explore various ways in which strengths may be developed, we now address an extremely important opportunity. It is the element that has possibly the highest potential to actually escalate a leader's strengths in the near term. Yet it is the one that we probably do least deliberately and least well and for which the least research has been conducted. It is the basic idea that valuable development can take place on the job and that work itself is a huge developmental opportunity if only managed properly.

Setting the Goal of Becoming an Excellent Leader

The realm of developing leadership skills includes one special challenge. The great majority of leaders begin their careers in some area of specialty. The leader may have been a chemist, an accountant, a marketer, an operations manager, an IT specialist, or a lawyer. The technical education of these leaders was usually focused in their area of specialty. Their career aspirations were most often to excel in the career of their choice. Assuming they had thought about their career in the long term, chances are they wanted to be the best possible chemical engineer or software programmer, or whatever their career choice had been.

In all likelihood, they never gave much thought to the idea that "as my career progresses, I will shift my aspirations away from my technical specialty and focus them on becoming an exceptional leader." The need to acquire a high level of leadership skills is usually an afterthought. It frequently comes at a later point in their career development. Their leadership skills have been acquired by observing and mimicking the bosses they've had to date. There may have been some limited formal development experiences, but normally these are relatively minimal. They acquire the skills required to perform at an adequate level through on-the-job training and experience. Often, depending on their area of specialty, they continued to spend a good part of their day in the technical area in which they were trained, and only part of their day is spent in leadership activities.

A portion of people who studied some technical or professional discipline took some business-oriented courses while in college or returned to school in an evening program that included business subjects. The great bulk of these courses are targeted to what we'll call management: finance, accounting, operations, marketing, risk management, or information technology. A tiny fraction of courses offered by colleges and universities deal with leadership. Those courses that do focus on leadership tend to be academic and theoretical; that is, they are about the subject of leadership, but they do not pretend to teach someone how to lead. Educational institutions are mainly about knowledge and information, not about building skills.

Several years ago one of the authors did some research looking at the strengths and weaknesses of leaders and matching them to their direct reports. In many cases it was found that leaders with profound strengths in particular competencies would have direct reports with the same strengths. Leaders with profound weaknesses would have direct reports with the same weaknesses. This phenomenon occurred more frequently than random chance would dictate, and we called it the "shadow of the leader." Just the process of being around and associating with a leader can cause people to acquire some of the leader's habits. The problem is that people pick up both good and bad habits. Some people have the opportunity to work for exceptional leaders, and those interactions help them to develop amazing skills. Unfortunately, many people never have an opportunity to work directly for leaders who are excellent role models.

Building Development into Your Job

It has been known for decades that altering the nature and content of a job could increase the satisfaction and overall motivation of people performing it. In the 1950s, Frederick Herzberg[1] researched job enlargement (adding more activities to a job) and job enrichment (increasing the challenge of work tasks). His theories were most often applied to frontline workers; his emphasis was not on managers and executives. Job enrichment and job enlargement were shown to improve the productivity of frontline workers. In addition, these practices enhanced overall employee satisfaction, and in turn, that led to higher employee retention.

These ideas have been extended and given a modern twist at the University of Michigan, where the term *job crafting* is used.[2] The basic idea is to focus on how workers at all levels can shape their jobs to add meaning and fulfillment. Job redesign can also be used as a leadership development tool by helping any workers, along with their manager, to identify opportunities for developmental activities that can be integrated into their current positions.

It has become almost an article of faith that the single most powerful tool for leadership development is the day-to-day work activities of the leader. There have been many references to the idea that a great deal of what leaders learn comes to them casually and informally from their daily work activities. In an earlier chapter, we noted the oft-quoted statistic describing how people learn on the job. It has been argued that on-the-job development comes from a 70-20-10 split, with 70 percent of learning coming from ongoing work experiences, 20 percent from coaching, and 10 percent from formal learning events such as seminars and workshops. (We noted earlier that this idea came from the pooled opinions of 30 executives in a seminar in response to a question about where and how they had gained their leadership skill. We suggest that you take the precise numbers with many grains of salt. We believe, however, that the general concept is valid.)

That work assignments play an important role in development is beyond debate. Over the years, many organizations have had great success in developing future executives by giving them demanding assignments. A favorite has been an overseas assignment in which an executive became a country manager and had all the functions of the business reporting to him or her. Another developmental assignment would be the responsibility of opening a new plant, with all the complexity that presents. The reason for moving executives from one functional area to another, and back and forth between line positions and staff functions, has been to get greater breadth and depth of experience that prepared the person for more senior positions. The point is simply that the process of using actual job assignments for developmental purposes is neither revolutionary nor new.

Ways to Build Learning into Ongoing Work Activity

We move now to exploring some specific ways that work can be used for the development of people in the organization. The first step is relatively simple. Leaders can take a thoughtful look at their current role in the organization. Leaders and managers have a certain degree of latitude regarding how they define and execute their job. They can choose where to spend more time and where to put emphasis. (However, we're in no way suggesting that they have a blank sheet of paper and complete freedom to choose what not to do and what to do.) The fact of the matter is, however, that two people coming into the same position will go about it somewhat differently. There is some degree of freedom about how every leadership role is structured. The leader can add some activities, take away other activities, and allocate time to those activities that would help in his or her ongoing development.

Action Learning as One Way of Building Leadership Strengths

Next we suggest some activities that are specifically designed to bring learning onto the job in a more formal way. The first has broadly been labeled *action learning*.

If you surveyed a group of leading corporations and asked about the major components of their overall leadership development efforts, one of the most frequently cited elements would be action learning. This approach was originally pioneered by Reginald Revans, a professor at the University of Manchester in England.[3] It began with his work in the coal mining industry in England, and his work spread from there.

The essence of the action learning concept is that we all learn by doing and that business leaders are no different. Revans's university had sponsored a variety of programs for executives, and he observed the impact the programs were having on participants. To his dismay, Revans became convinced that the programs were having little or no impact. It became clear to Revans that the conventional methods of teaching hardly made a dent on the way leaders behaved. Knowledge and information did not change behavior. Increasingly he came to believe that rather than have leaders study the usual abstractions about management (such as planning, organizing, control, or strategy), it was best to have them study their own actions at work, along with how they were experiencing their work. He was convinced that the best course content was the actual work they were performing.

In addition, his belief was that leaders learned best when they worked together in teams, tackling real strategic or major tactical problems the organization faced, then posing fresh questions and being open to new and different points of view. Learning was accelerated when the team members were encouraged to share their own biases about the questions and to define their mental models to one another.

The purpose of action learning was exactly what the term implied. There was no learning without action, and no action that was well thought out would occur without significant learning taking place. Therefore, action enhances learning, and learning enhances action. The philosophy worked when the senior-most leaders were willing to engage with others in taking a fresh look at big issues.

One element that seems to be key in the action learning process is the willingness of top management to identify serious problems. Asking action learning teams to focus on fixing issues that have little impact can never provide enough interest or payoff for plans to be implemented. Once a significant problem is identified, it is critical that leaders who are responsible for the problem area be willing to take the risk of attempting to fix the problem. It is important that they be willing to grant sufficient authority to the action learning team to fix the problem and enable the team to implement its recommendations.

Another critical element is that once the implementation is complete, the action learning team take the time to extract what it learned from the activity. This is rarely done in most work settings because people generally move on to new priorities without taking the time to crystallize what they learned.

The key to the success of action learning from our perspective is the degree to which the learning process becomes deliberate, explicit, and planned. It cannot be left to chance. Reflection time needs to accompany the implementation of solutions. While Revans did not support having a facilitator appointed to ensure that learning was occurring, others who have applied this idea have done just that. Indeed, we believe that the majority of firms today use a facilitator-consultant whose job it to observe and help the group to identify key learnings. The facilitator-consultant will work with action learning teams to ensure that learning is keeping pace with the actions being taken.

In practice, senior leaders in firms identify a key problem for action learning teams to solve. Group members are given time off from their normal activities to define the problem more fully, to gather data, to explore solutions, to implement their solution, and throughout this process to periodically discuss what they are learning about themselves and each other.

If the task assigned to the group was vital to the organization's future and if the topic is highly complex, the time demands can interfere with or detract from current work assignments. Today, many organizations are selecting topics for action learning projects that are more directly linked to the participants' current work. Knowing the ever-increasing pressures that most of today's leaders face, we believe that this is an important refinement to the action learning process.

After-Action Reviews as a Means of Building Strengths Development into Work

Another method for building learning into work is a technique pioneered by the military. The idea was rather simple. At the conclusion of every mission, the group who participated in the event would be assembled for an after-action review (AAR). The ground rule was that all the participants in the room would take off their stripes (not always literally, but psychologically), with the intent of making everyone equal in the discussion. A facilitator would be selected whose job was to draw out answers, insights, and any unspoken issues. This person was to make sure that the climate allowed everyone to speak and that the process did not devolve into finger-pointing or blaming. Normally the facilitator would be someone who had been marginally involved in the project or mission and seldom would have been a key participant.

The process began with a review of the original objectives of the mission. The questions would be:

- What did we set out to do? (What were the objectives?)
- What actually happened?
- What went well?
- What could have gone better?
- What would we do differently next time?
- What did we learn?

Further comments can amplify this simple framework. The objective was to identify what went well and to ensure that those actions would be repeated in the future. Notice the strong emphasis on what could broadly be labeled as strengths, rather than placing the major focus on weaknesses. Only after exploring what went well would the focus turn to "What could have gone better?" Note that the question was not "What went wrong?" This way the group can learn from more than just mistakes—they can learn from anything that could have gone better. The emphasis is on continual improvement, not failure. The key question was to keep focusing on what you might do differently next time as a way of learning from every mission.

A helpful technique used by some facilitators is to ask each member of the group for a numerical rating of the project: "Looking back, how satisfied are you with the project? Give it a mark on a scale from 1 to 10." People who said the project was fine might still score it an 8, which prompts the facilitator to ask, "What would have made it a 10 for you?" This leads to a discussion of what could have gone better.

Someone is asked to keep minutes of the AAR to ensure that the conclusions are not forgotten. This often falls to the facilitator.

Identifying Role Models

As noted earlier, many of us have never had the good fortune to work for an outstanding leader. Given the fact that outstanding leaders are in short supply, it should not come as a surprise. Statistically, the odds are against having that happen. If we work for a good-sized organization, however, there's a far better likelihood that somewhere in the organization you can identify leaders who possess powerful strengths and who are individuals from whom you can learn a great deal. Some organizations establish formal mentoring programs, but those organizations are the exception, not the rule. Nothing prevents us from seeking out high-performing leaders and asking for their counsel about handling various situations. We've seldom heard of senior leaders turning down a request from an obviously sincere, aspiring leader who asked for some time to discuss career issues or some challenging situation the person was facing. If you happen to be in a company with an official mentoring program, by all means raise your hand and volunteer to be a participant. While much learning on the job is unstructured, informal, unplanned, and spur-of-the-moment, that does not mean that you cannot work to make more of it happen more of the time.

Start with Selecting a Competency You Seek to Develop

Building development opportunities into your job starts with selecting a competency to develop that is aligned with what your organization and team needs and for which you have energy and enthusiasm. Development activities that directly support performance goals tend to receive the most time and attention. Chapter 6 addressed this topic in greater detail.

It's also often possible to modify the collection of organizational tasks that make up your current job in a way that still meets organization and team needs and at the same time provides additional opportunities for development of your chosen competency. Let us now take the concept of nonlinear development that we described in Chapter 4 and combine it with the creation of opportunities for development within the job that we are performing.

CASE STUDY: JENNIFER SEEKS TO BECOME A MORE INSPIRING LEADER

Based on the data we have available from the thousands of participants in our leadership development programs, the most frequently selected target for development based on our experience to date is *inspires and motivates others to high performance*. Let's begin by reviewing the competency companions for this competency of inspiring and motivating shown in Figure 9.1.

Figure 9.1 Ten Competency Companions That Help Leaders Inspire and Motivate Others

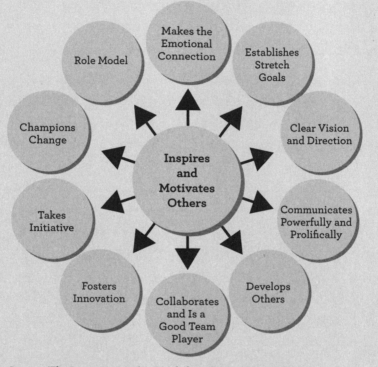

Source: The Inspiring Leader Workshop © 2010 Zenger Folkman

Let's assume that Jennifer has decided that she wishes to be more inspiring and has reviewed this list of 10 companion behaviors. After starting at 12 o'clock and going around the circle, she has decided that three of these companion behaviors hold out promise for her. The ones she selects are:

1. Establishes stretch goals

(continues)

(continued)

2. Communicates powerfully and prolifically

3. Develops others

She now determines that she will find a way to build these into her job in the coming quarter of the year. The following might represent some specific actions that Jennifer would schedule for herself.

1. *Establishes stretch goals.* Jennifer's team functions adequately but has not risen to the level that Jennifer had hoped for when she took it over two years ago. She is convinced that the processes the team uses have become antiquated and could be streamlined. So her first step is to ask the team members to consider a goal for significantly improving their work processes. Jennifer believes the processes could be improved by at least 25 percent. She wants the members of the team to participate in deciding to take this project on, and she certainly wants their buy-in for the specific improvement objective. She also wants them to agree on how long it will take, as well as the resources they will need to pull this off. Her plan is to explain that they can't hire any outside help, but must fit the project into the ongoing work they are doing. Her decision to do this is driven by a lack of budget for outside resources and also her belief that the time spent in educating an outside consultant would probably be roughly equal to the time they would spend in doing the analysis and coming up with recommendations for improved processes. Jennifer believes that a challenging assignment can unify the members of the group and energize them as long as they feel ownership for it.

2. *Communicates powerfully and prolifically.* Jennifer senses that decisions made in her leadership team meetings are not being communicated consistently or accurately to the entire workforce. Her solution is to produce a simple, home-made webinar in which she along with the assistant manager of the group would talk about the decisions that have been made in the meeting. She will also use these occasions to review the current strategy. "Frankly," she muses, "I'm getting sick of repeating this message, but every really successful executive I know says that I should give that speech every time I meet with a group of our employees. So I'll give that speech as often as possible." She's also considering getting a colleague to videotape short segments of her interviewing various work teams about their significant accomplishments and then having those sent on the company intranet to all employees. At the end of the quarter, her plan is to send out a short survey asking people for their reaction to some of these new communication initiatives.

3. *Develops others.* Jennifer has six people who report directly to her. She is genuinely interested in their career progress, but she realizes that they would have no tangible way of knowing that. So she commits to herself that she will do the following, all in the coming quarter.

a. She will meet with each direct report and include in that conversation a detailed discussion of this person's career aspirations. Jennifer realizes that she can't do a great deal about helping in the development process unless she knows what each one aspires to do and what kind of developmental opportunities the person would like to have.

(continues)

(continued)

b. She will schedule coaching conversations with each of her direct reports. One person, in particular, shows huge potential. However, this person also has some rough edges, and her hope had been that time would smooth those over. That has not happened, and she now needs to step up and provide some honest feedback, along with offering time for some coaching sessions to all her direct reports. She knows she owes that to them.

c. She has observed that her subordinates fill in the box on the annual performance review that describes their personal development plan but that no one follows through on that. Worse yet, she has not followed through either. There are no consequences, neither rewards nor punishments, if someone succeeds or fails at following through. She wants to change that and will tell her subordinates that she feels as strongly about their proceeding with their plans as she does about their completing projects on time and on budget.

d. She also recognizes that she has not identified developmental activities for each of her people, budgeted for the activities, or scheduled her people's attendance at such programs. She knows this needs to change.

If Jennifer does these things in the coming quarter, she will be working on the development of her own leadership strengths, and these are all activities that are part of her ongoing work. They fit into the chinks of her busy workday; and she knows that if she pulls them off, not only will she be a better leader, but her work group will be the huge beneficiary of her taking the initiative to become more effective.

How to Make Learning Easy

On a recent trip to Amsterdam one of the authors was discussing with a local person how well almost everyone in the Netherlands spoke English. The author was curious about what was done to bring this all about. The local person mentioned that English was taught in all the schools from an early age and that because not that many people in the world speak Dutch, most people in the Netherlands realize the value of having a second or third language. The local then said, "I also think that television had a substantial impact." The author was curious and asked, "You mean English-as-a-second-language shows broadcast on TV helped?" The local replied, "Oh, no, that did not help at all. They started showing English sitcoms that people enjoyed watching. They learned English while they laughed at the comedy." So often when we meet a leader who possesses an amazing skill we ask, "How did you learn that skill?" The most common answer is, "I was assigned a new job that forced me to learn the skill, it was sink or swim; it took some time and effort but eventually I become very good at the skill."

If you want to learn a skill, then build that skill into your job. Find opportunities to practice the skill on your job. Ask for feedback on what went well and what you could do better. Over time, if you were to take a before and after video, you would be very surprised to see how much you have improved.

Sustaining Strengths

Building Follow-Through into Your Development Plan

Another key to success in developing a strength is extensive fol-low-through. People don't win the 100-yard dash by running extremely well for 50 yards and then coasting. What do we know about creating sustainability and follow-through?

Formula for Sustainability

Let us propose a formula:

Sustainability = learner's motivation × clarity of
the goal × support from others × opportunities
for practice × measurement of progress

We have deliberately placed multiplication symbols between each of the elements. This means that if any one of these elements is a zero, the outcome, no matter how large the other elements, will be zero.

Let's review each of the components to understand why we'd take such a strong stand on the importance of each.

Learner's Motivation and Readiness

Strengths are developed when people have a strong desire to cultivate a particular trait or quality. They believe that the skill can be acquired and that they will be able to use it in their work. Such motivation is extremely difficult to give to anyone else. It is self-generated. In Daniel Pink's book *Drive,* he presents compelling evidence that our traditional beliefs about what motivates people are outmoded and incorrect. In a nutshell, he argues that our beliefs about people being motivated primarily by monetary rewards or fear of punishment simply are not accurate. The carrot and stick are no longer valid conceptions of motivation. They may work to a small degree in special circumstances, but the truly powerful motivators are autonomy, mastery of one's work, and a strong purpose that gives work a deeper meaning.

Two elements are important. First, you must obviously be motivated if there is to be a sustained effort to develop a strength. Determination and stick-to-itiveness are essential. Second, linking your efforts to the genuine elements of motivation will escalate success. If the skill you've chosen gives you greater autonomy in your work, a higher sense of mastery in what you are doing, and the sense that you are working toward a higher cause or purpose, this will clearly expand your motivation.

CASE STUDY

A young, aspiring leader has decided to work on increasing the level of initiative that she displays. Her motivation

(continues)

(continued)

is fairly clear to her. She is a person who doesn't like others telling her what to do or how to do it. In discussing this fact with her boss, he suggested that one way to minimize that happening was for her to grab the ball and run with it, not waiting to be told what to do at every turn. He suggested looking about and seeing what needed to be done or what could be done that would greatly improve the quality of the output from the work team. He suggested that this was clearly one way to minimize being directed by others and to have greater autonomy in her job. Fortunately, that same activity would also give her a greater sense of mastery over her work. She would feel herself to be ahead of the curve, and she would actually be more on top of things.

The reality of motivation is that it lies within the individual. It cannot be mysteriously injected into a subordinate at the will of the manager, anymore than it can be implanted into a teenager by a concerned parent. We can create the environment in which motivation is more likely to be unleashed. Pink's research on the impact of autonomy, mastery of work, and work having higher meaning are the key ingredients of a truly motivating environment.

Goal Clarity

Persistence in developing a strength hinges on knowing how you will use it and what specific steps are required to put this strength into place. Leaders who aspire to be better at strategic thinking must see the importance of this skill and how it can be applied in the course of their work. They must also understand what the skill looks like in practice. It cannot be obtuse or vague.

Practice that leads to better performance calls for a person to do something new and challenging with an improvement goal in mind.

CASE STUDY

If a person goes out once a week and plays golf exactly the same way he had been playing in the past months, it is virtually certain that he will stay exactly at the same skill level. To change requires deliberate practice. As we noted earlier in the book, the aspiring golfer who wants to truly improve lays out on the grass some large circles made of white tape at various distances. Then the golfer attempts to hit buckets of balls into the closest circle until a high percentage of them successfully land in it. The golfer then begins aiming for the next furthest circle out using the same process. The golfer continues in this fashion, increasing the skills of direction and distance control. This is deliberate practice. Contrast that with going out to a driving range and blissfully hitting buckets full of balls. Although that effort may be enjoyable (especially on a beautiful day), it's unlikely to make little, if any, difference in the skill levels of most people. It is only when the goal is clear and challenging that practice takes on genuine meaning.

Support from Others

The environment that surrounds a leader is complex. It starts with the culture of the organization. It includes the roles of the immediate manager, the peers, and the subordinates of the leader involved. It might also include a coach or mentor, and it could often include a concerned HR leader whose goal is to assist in the development of leaders in the organization.

CASE STUDY

Craig is a manager of a large department. The organization sees real potential in him and tells him that he has a bright future if he will continue to develop himself. So who is responsible for Craig's efforts to develop his strengths? Is it the HR executive? Is it Craig's manager? Or is it Craig? This can feel like the Bermuda Triangle of Vanishing Accountability. Each of these people can point to the others and say, "Yes, I know I'm responsible in some way, but I'm not fully accountable."

The manager says, "No one ever said that it was my responsibility to ensure that Craig developed leadership strengths. That's between HR and Craig. Sure, I'm interested and want to help, but I've got eight other direct reports."

The HR leader's position is, "My job is to provide learning opportunities, coaching, and feedback, but this is the line manager's and the participant's responsibility. HR's role is an advisory one. We have no power or authority to make things happen."

The participant muses, "Well, I know that this is about me, and I obviously am responsible for my development to a large degree; but my manager doesn't seem to notice if I improve the way I lead. The manager only cares about the numbers. It is the results and not the means that upper management worries about. There's never any discussion about the progress I'm making on my development. Yes, there's a box on the annual performance appraisal form, but no one takes that seriously. Also, I have no way of knowing if I'm getting better. I get no feedback. Working here is like being in a coal mine with no lights on. I don't see the rewards for

getting a lot better at communicating with my people. Communication is not coming down to me, and furthermore . . ."
(You get the picture.)

The environment can play a huge role in whether or not a leader develops strengths. Yes, we believe it is primarily Craig's responsibility. However, the others, especially the manager, have very strong roles to play in Craig's success in developing his strengths. The manager's ongoing coaching can have a major effect. HR can provide processes (repeated 360-degree feedback) and other channels (coaching) to help the leader have ample feedback. For real sustainability to occur, all the components of the environment—boss, peers, subordinates, and HR—need to work together to support Craig's development.

Opportunities for Practice

Leadership strengths, as we have chosen to define them, are largely skills and behaviors. They are not inner attitudes and feelings. Nor are they thought processes taking place inside someone's head. While they may begin as thoughts, they become expressed in certain behaviors that invariably involve others.

Someone could argue that the competency of problem solving is largely a cerebral, personal process. The research, however, would show that problem solving is a set of complex behaviors that begin with:

- Identifying a problem, usually by obtaining data from others
- Defining those issues creating or contributing to the problem, often with the help of others
- Walking around the problem and collecting more information with the help of others

- Identifying alternative solutions, again often with the help of others
- Examining the likely outcomes for each solution, again with the help of others
- Selecting the best alternative and then planning for its implementation

It is true that an occasional problem-solving activity may occur with one person in a room all by herself, but most problem-solving activities in companies are complex and interconnected and definitely involve other people. What started out as a cerebral activity quickly becomes highly interpersonal and inclusive of many others.

Acquiring skills requires practice, both to learn the skill and to cement it into place as a guarantee of retention. Practice is also required if the person is to get better. As our golf example highlighted earlier, practice doesn't make perfect. Deliberate, perfect practice is the only thing that makes perfect.

Many of these opportunities for practice will come from on-the-job experiences, as described earlier in Chapter 9. Further opportunities for practice may come from activities in the community, service organizations, trade associations, charities, or religious groups.

Measurement of Progress

If Craig is going to sustain his efforts, he needs some way to determine if progress is being made. We know of no better way of doing this than via a repeat 360-degree feedback process. This process provides an objective, relatively comprehensive view, showing whether or not the desired trait is being strengthened. The 360 is reasonably quantitative, and it is repeatable over time.

When the 360-degree feedback process is repeated, the results can be used to generate a "gap" report. The idea is to lay the earlier and later 360 reports side by side and to look for the existence of gaps—

analyzing areas in which the individual may have improved, stayed the same, or declined in scores. In addition, knowing at the beginning of the development process that there will be future rounds of 360 data collected provides a level of accountability and further incentive for diligent follow-on and practice.

Various software solutions are available that offer a way for people to track activities around developmental goals, to record specific activities being undertaken, to assess progress being made, and to track overall movement. Microsoft Outlook has many of the features required to do this. Other software packages have been created specifically to monitor and measure progress.

Follow-on Activities

A wide range of options exist to extend learning. Some of these include:

1. Asking participants to write a follow-up letter or an e-mail to the facilitator regarding actions taken and results achieved

2. Periodic telephone calls to check in and report on activities

3. Scheduled meetings with a manager or coach

4. Surveys sent out by the facilitator to collect information about successful implementations

5. Additional group sessions scheduled periodically after an initial learning event

Conclusion

Success in this process of follow-through does not come from doing these things haphazardly or sporadically. Nor does it usually come from doing them sequentially. It comes when they are put into place concurrently. We return to our formula with the various elements being multiplied, not added to one another. We're convinced that if any one of the elements is missing, the result will be zero.

Special
Considerations

Chapter 11 proposes that working on strengths is not something just for managers or leaders, but that it pertains equally to individual contributors, who are the professional backbone of every organization.

Chapter 12 explores the distinction between weaknesses and fatal flaws and discusses the appropriate course of action that people should take when they have one versus the other.

Chapter 13 takes issue with a commonly held belief that strengths can be taken too far. It contends that genuine strengths can never be practiced in excess.

Chapter 14 describes the power and value of multi-rater feedback, or what is commonly described as 360-degree feedback, as a tool for building strengths. It presents the characteristics of the best of these instruments.

Individual Contributors

Building on Strengths Is the Foundation of Success at Every Level

I t's often assumed that leadership is an assignment strictly for super-visors, managers, and executives. These are people who have been placed into formal positions of power and designated to provide leadership for the organization. They presumably are seen as the ones who have the foresight needed to identify and drive new initiatives, the authority to make decisions, and the trappings of power needed to get people to follow their lead. The rest of the workforce, consisting of nonmanagerial workers and staff personnel, also known as individual contributors, are all supposed to be followers, not leaders.

In this chapter we suggest an alternative perspective on the definition of leadership, who demonstrates it, and how it is executed within an organization. We assert that individual contributors can potentially be leaders and have the opportunity to use their influence to make a difference with an organization. Not only that, our productivity research shows that organizations today, more than ever, need these individuals to help lead those organizations so that key targets and results can be attained. A final focus of this chapter is to look at how a "building-on-strengths" approach to development is essential to the ongoing success of individual contributors.

There have been many examples of great leaders who were not in formal positions of power in their organizations. Individuals who didn't control huge financial budgets, manage and direct the work of large teams, or determine strategy. Yet, as individual contributors, their actions made a big difference. Similar to leaders with positional authority, individual contributors have the ability to see opportunities or potential problems, show initiative when needed, and lead others in the accomplishment of important objectives. Despite the numerous examples of the difference these folks make, their leadership contributions aren't always apparent. Sometimes this is due to the accomplishment of their work product being attributed to the "boss." Or, the work is seen as a team effort, and the magnitude of the individual contributor's work isn't completely understood. Yet, it is the leadership efforts shown by these individuals that produce successful outcomes. The following example represents one such individual contributor who wasn't in a formal leadership position, yet his actions had a significant impact on the organization.

STORY 1

Eric Knightly, Technical Support

Eric Knightly worked as a technical specialist for a leading software firm and provided technical support to the marketing department as one of his responsibilities. The organization was preparing to announce a major product update to more than 1.5 million users for its flagship product. The announcement letter was given to Eric, and he was responsible for getting it distributed within 72 hours.

While preparing the letter for distribution, Eric noticed the letter contained some ambiguities, which he knew could easily be misinterpreted by customers. He was pretty certain that the letter would raise more questions than provide answers and, if sent as written, would potentially result in the call center being flooded with calls from anxious customers concerned about how they would be affected by the impending product update. Eric took the initiative and contacted his firm's marketing vice president to discuss the letter, as he wanted to help prevent this risk of fallout and protect the firm's reputation from negative publicity. He thought the marketing department could easily make the corrections and that he could still get the letter distributed by the original deadline. The marketing VP thanked Eric for expressing his concern and, to his surprise, still wanted the letter distributed without any suggested changes. Eric was taken aback by the marketing VP's decision and tried to convince him to reconsider. The marketing VP refused and directed Eric to send the letter.

After some reflection, Eric went to his manager, showed him the letter, and asked what action could be taken to get the letter corrected before being distributed. Eric's manager suggested that they review the situation with their manager, the chief technology officer, and see what he'd advise. The CTO thanked both Eric and the manager for bringing the letter to his attention and said he'd follow up with them in a few days. He said the letter wouldn't be able to be sent by the original deadline and that he would take responsibility for delaying its distribution. The CTO, unbeknownst to his staff members, decided to escalate the situation to the CEO and have him make the final decision about the impending communication. The CEO later called a meeting with the CTO, Eric, and Eric's manager regarding the letter. The CEO thanked them for taking the appropriate steps that led to the matter being escalated to his attention. He acknowledged their professionalism and expressed appreciation for not only the pride shown in their work but also for their commitment level to the firm's success. He informed them that the letter would be corrected and that he and the CTO would ensure this would not result in bad blood between technical support and the marketing team.

While Eric is an individual contributor and lacked positional authority, he took action that he felt was in the best interest of the organization. He showed initiative by reading a letter that wasn't required of his role and was prepared to face any consequences that could have resulted if upper management hadn't supported his position. Eric could have taken an easier course of action. He could have decided not to speak up and allow the letter to be sent as he was originally instructed. This certainly would have hurt the firm's reputation. Still, upon review of the incident, Eric wouldn't have been held accountable for the mishap, as detecting the issue of the letter's content wasn't part of his job description. Eric had more at stake by speaking up than by keeping quiet. Nevertheless, Eric chose to be a leader in the situation and exercised his influence. It was the best decision for the firm at the time, and his actions played a significant role in ensuring a successful outcome.

When it comes to the concept of individual contributors as leaders and the consideration of their achievements, like an Eric Knightly, two facts are easily observed: 1) high performers are willing to make unique differences to their organizations, and 2) they don't meet the traditional definition of organizational leaders having great "positional power." As illustrated by Knightly, individual contributors make important contributions yet they do it without carrying management titles that suggest high organizational rank, authority, or prestige. They, like Knightly, influence and inspire others without being in roles of *assigned leadership*. For individual contributors working in organizations today and for those responsible to develop them professionally, this raises four important questions:

1. Can individual contributors be leaders?

2. What elements contribute to the high performance of individual contributors?

3. How much of an impact can highly effective individual contributors have?

4. In an organization, is the process for developing individual contributors different from that for developing traditional leaders?

Question 1. Can Individual Contributors Really Be Expected to Lead Others?

The terms *individual* and *leadership* together sound like an oxymoron. By definition, it might appear that a precondition to being a leader is the need to have others to lead. So to what degree can individual contributors without direct reports be considered leaders?

The argument against individual contributors being considered leaders would be that they lack rank or power that confers authority to make decisions and commit an organization. They don't control budget resources to fund organizational activities, and—most noticeably—they aren't responsible for leading a team. The argument would be that such individuals may be contributing good things but still aren't leaders if their roles haven't been formally sanctioned by the organization.

The opposite argument, and one we believe to be true, is that individual contributors can be leaders and demonstrate their leadership capability on behalf of the organization when needed. We would argue that a leader isn't limited to those with positional authority. Leadership instead would be defined alternatively as *someone who influences others to achieve a common goal*. This would represent the work and contributions of anyone who serves in this capacity.

When Individual Contributors Become Leaders

With an expanded definition of leadership, it's easier to identify the countless people who perform in this manner, that is, lead others without titles, positions, or organizational status.

People like Eric Knightly who don't possess corner offices or have annual performance bonuses, stock options, and expense accounts motivating them to high performance while acting on behalf of the company's best interest. Since their contributions mirror that of traditional leaders, should they, too, be considered leaders, and should their ongoing development be approached accordingly? Based on some research we conducted, we determined every organization needs people to assume *leadership* roles when opportunities arise. We will provide evidence of the tremendous impact individuals can have on organizational results when they exercise their leadership ability.

Question 2. What Elements Contribute to the High Performance of Individual Contributors?

In Chapter 6, we described the CPO model and explained its usefulness in determining which strengths would be good candidates for leaders to further develop. Let's use the CPO model here in a slightly different way, this time to better understand how individual contributors can achieve high levels of performance. Those performing at high levels generally demonstrate capability in each of the model's three areas.

They're Competent (C)

They demonstrate high skill levels in areas that matter to their jobs. This is important because there is a large body of evidence that indicates highly skilled people make greater contributions because they're significantly more productive. For example, Hunter, Schmidt, and Judiesch summarized a variety of different studies on the impact of individual skills and productivity. They found that in medium-complexity jobs (such as team leads, bookkeepers, machinists) those individuals whose skills were in the top 1 percent were on average 85 percent more productive than those whose skills were in the 50th percentile and 12 times more productive that the lowest-performing individual. In high-complexity jobs (such as software engineers, sales leaders, executives, lawyers, CPAs), they found that those with skills in the top 1 percent were 127 percent more productive than those with skills at the 50th percentile and infinitely more productive than the lowest-ranking person in a distribution of 100. Figure 11.1 depicts the results.

They're Passionate (P)

They demonstrate zeal, interest, and a willingness to practice the skills important in the job. This is vital because of the large amount of time and effort required to develop skills to a high level. Research on the development of expertise in a variety of domains (such as memory, sports, chess, music, mathematical calculations) has shown that exceptional performers demonstrate an unusual passion for developing a skill when trying to master it. It was mentioned earlier in Chapter 6

Figure 11.1 Relative Job Complexity

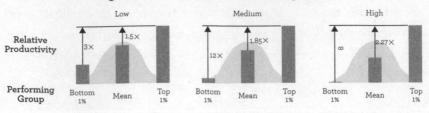

that long periods of dedicated practice—along with the motivation and time required to perform it—were essential to become an expert in most domains.

Researchers John Wilding and Elizabeth Valentine studied individuals with an unusual level of memory ability to recall a prior fact, event, or visual representation.[1] They found that their subjects' motivation and interest in becoming exceptional was, at the least, equally as important as their natural recall ability and sometimes more important. In fact, their research shows that in nearly all cases of memory superiority, the experts depended on special techniques, strategies, and practice—requiring high levels of passion and interest—more than any unusual level of innate talent.

Charles Darwin reflected on the importance of passion in the development of an ability when he said, "Excepting fools, men did not differ much in intellect, only in zeal and hard work."[2]

They Understand What's Needed in the Organization (O)

They are organizationally aware and understand where they can contribute to have a big impact. Whether it's the result of an innate "environmental scanning" ability, an ongoing and genuine interest in what's going on in the workplace, or the felt need to regularly seek feedback from others, high-performing individual contributors are often looking outside their own needs to understand what efforts could help the organization around them.

Together with their competence in skills that are important to the job and their passion for exceptional performance, high-performing individual contributors have an organizational awareness for what needs to be done that helps them contribute in ways that significantly matter.

Question 3. How Much of an Impact Can Highly Effective Individual Contributors Have?

We've assessed over 2,000 individual contributors who have participated in a 180-degree multi-rater survey where they were given feedback by their managers, peers, and customers and also rated themselves. The raters were asked to evaluate each participant's effectiveness against the 16 differentiating competencies.

The results of the surveys were then compared against separate measures of (1) how productive the participants were perceived to be and (2) how much effort they were seen as putting into their work. The assessments of individual productivity and effort were supplied by each participant's direct manager.

The results were striking. Figures 11.2 and 11.3 depict a strong statistical correlation between how effective individual contributors are perceived to be and what those same individuals' levels of productivity and effort are as observed by their managers.

There is obviously a strong link between effort and productivity (Figure 11.2). This is equally as true for individual contributors as it is for managers and executives. Any individual contributor who chooses to put forth focused and intensive effort can see that result in greater productivity, which translates into perceived overall effectiveness.

Note in this study that individual contributors who are rated at the 1st through the 9th percentile in overall effectiveness have productivity ratings that are at only the 11th percentile, but those rated at the

Figure 11.2 Effectiveness Versus Productivity

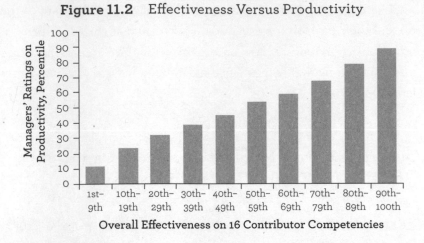

90th through 100th percentile are viewed as being at the 89th percentile in terms of their productivity. Roughly the same results occur when comparing overall perceived effectiveness with the individual contributors' levels of effort (Figure 11.3). What we conclude is that there is a strong link between perceived effectiveness in these 16 behaviors and observed productivity and effort levels. The same traits and behaviors that were identified as the 16 most powerful, differentiating competen-

Figure 11.3 Effectiveness Versus Effort

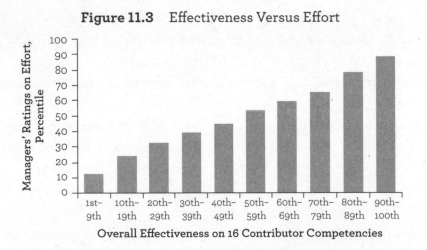

cies for those in managerial roles were also virtually parallel with those that differentiated the high-performing individual contributors.

Question 4. In an Organization, Is the Process for Developing Individual Contributors Different from That for Developing Traditional Managers and Leaders?

The short answer is no. Individual contributors wanting to become better leaders will benefit from the same strengths-based approach to development as those leaders who are in more formal managerial roles. The approach involves:

- Assessing the individual's competencies to identify strengths and potential fatal flaws
- Identifying high-impact strengths to build (or fatal flaws to first fix)
- Using a traditional linear approach to fixing any fatal flaws
- Using a nonlinear approach to building the selected strengths

In our research work, we've contrasted assessment data from the most successful and the least successful individual contributors. The results of this analysis revealed the following 16 competencies that best differentiate the most effective individual contributors from the rest:

Character
- Displays high integrity and honesty

Personal Capability
- Has technical or professional expertise
- Solves problems and analyzes issues

- Innovates
- Practices self-development

Focus on Results

- Drives for results
- Establishes stretch goals
- Takes initiative

Interpersonal Skills

- Communicates powerfully and prolifically
- Sets an example of high performance
- Builds relationships
- Develops others
- Engages in collaboration and teamwork

Leading Change

- Has broad perspectives
- Champions change
- Connects the group to the outside world—networking

You'll notice that these differentiating competencies for individual contributors are practically identical to those leader competencies described earlier in the book. Although the competency descriptions are similar, many of the specific behaviors have been adjusted to accommodate the differences in roles and responsibilities between formal managers and individual contributors.

As with managers who are in formal leadership roles, extraordinary individual contributors are differentiated by the existence of a few profound strengths, not the absence of weaknesses. They, too, should implement their development efforts using the same approach

Figure 11.4   Overall Effectiveness Versus Strengths

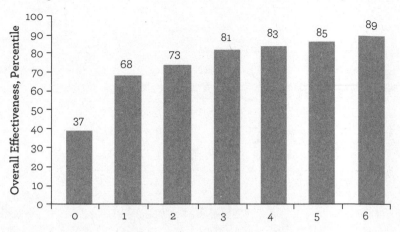

of building strengths rather than fixing weaknesses. Our point of view comes from the data in Figure 11.4. The data show that the overall effectiveness of an individual with three profound strengths is generally perceived as being in the 80th or higher percentile.

The same approach of utilizing nonlinear development to develop a strength, described in Chapter 4, works just as effectively with individual contributors as it does with managers and executives. Organizations that have begun providing 180 feedback and leadership development opportunities early in the careers of individual contributors have found not only that they prepare these people to become excellent managers in the future, but that their current effectiveness as individual contributors is greatly enhanced.

CHAPTER 12

Getting Out
of the Pit

When to Fix
Weaknesses and
Fatal Flaws

The Difference Between Weaknesses
and Fatal Flaws

As we talk to groups of leaders, it is interesting to ask the question, "How many of you think that just possibly you might have at least one weakness?" Of course, every hand goes up. Most people are well aware that they have some weaknesses. It is also a fascinating experience to ask people to think of the best leader they have ever worked with or closely observed. If you ask about this person's strengths, the answers come quickly. You can then ask, "Did this person have any weaknesses?" Once again the answer invariably is, "Yes—he [or she] was not perfect."

For some, it is an "aha" experience to understand that you do not need to be perfect to be an exceptional leader. No individuals have ever argued that they worked for, or had ever observed, a leader who was devoid of weaknesses. But while it's okay for leaders to have weaknesses, it needs to be understood that there is an enormous difference between a common weakness and a fatal flaw.

Statistically we think of a fatal flaw as a weakness at or below the 10th percentile (bottom 10 percent compared with others). Having this significant weakness most often counters or negates the positive impact of profound strengths. In every case we have examined, fatal flaws appear to pull down the effectiveness of a leader. These cases are not rare or unusual. Statistically we find that 28 percent of the population of leaders has one or more competencies at the 10th percentile or lower.

How Do You Identify a Fatal Flaw?

Our definition of a fatal flaw is a behavior or trait that has a devastatingly negative impact on a person's overall effectiveness. The statistical description or measure (10th percentile or lower) cannot be used as the sole criterion because certain behaviors are simply not important in a particular job. For example, a first-level supervisor may be rated at the 10th percentile on the competency of *develops strategic perspectives,* but this person may not need to be strategic in her thinking. Her role is to produce things on time, on budget, and with extremely high quality. Others are worrying about the strategy of the firm. Now, one might argue that the first-level supervisor is not likely to be promoted to a senior position in the company until she is viewed as being competent at strategic thinking. Therefore, this is in fact a fatal flaw when it comes to her opportunities for promotion.

An important element of a fatal flaw is that it is a behavior that is viewed as being very important in the person's current job or in the culture of the organization. In a professional services firm, technical expertise is so highly valued, that all the professional staff members need to be technically competent in order to keep their job.

One way to measure if a weakness is fatal is to note whether it is the first trait people think about when a person's name is mentioned. It becomes the filter through which all other traits are viewed. This filter colors all other characteristics. In many cases, people refuse to attribute any positive characteristics to a person because the fatal flaw has such a negative impact.

As we work with leaders who receive 360 feedback, this is a very important question they need to answer—"Do you have a fatal flaw?" Some people argue that our language may be too extreme or harsh, but we find that describing this in highly negative terms is helpful at getting people to understand the devastatingly negative impact of the behavior.

In the transition from poor to good leadership, focusing on fixing fatal flaws is essential. Leaders with fatal flaws will never be viewed as key talent in an organization. Figure 12.1 shows results from over 27,000 leaders. Note that leaders with three or more fatal flaws have an overall leadership effectiveness rating at the 11th percentile.

Figure 12.1 The Impact of Fatal Flaws on Overall Leadership Effectiveness

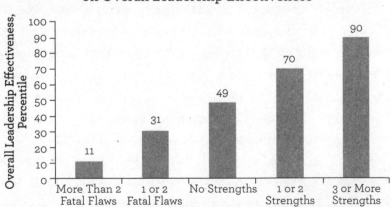

Leaders with just one or two fatal flaws are at the 31st percentile on their overall effectiveness, placing them into the bottom third of the distribution of leaders.

Fatal flaws have a devastating impact on the perception of a leader's overall effectiveness. Our advice for leaders with fatal flaws is to make a priority of fixing any fatal flaws first, before working on a strength. The good news is that with effort and attention, leaders can make a profound change in these negative issues. Typically, they do not move these fatal flaws all the way to having them become profound strengths, but they can move them to the point where they are an average capability. It is comforting to know that there are abundant data to support the fact that people can fix fatal flaws.

Impact of Fixing a Fatal Flaw

Let's reiterate the finding that a person with multiple fatal flaws has an overall effectiveness rating at the 17th percentile. The bottom line appears to be that the fatal flaw simply craters the person's effectiveness. When people have a fatal flaw, others tend to view negatively not just the fatal flaw, but all their behaviors and traits—it's a spillover effect where perceptions are strongly contaminated by the fatal flaw.

Our advice for people with fatal flaws is to immediately take steps to fix them. The really good news is that addressing a fatal flaw can have a substantial positive impact on how these people are perceived.

In studying the impact of fixing fatal flaws, we looked at the pretest versus posttest results for 80 leaders. In this study, we found 15 leaders who had one or more competencies that were in the fatal flaws category as defined by the statistic of being in the bottom decile. We found that 11 of the 15 leaders with fatal flaws made significant positive progress by focusing on fixing their fatal flaws. In the pretest results, the average effectiveness rating for the 11 leaders was the 20th percentile. The posttest results indicated that working hard and addressing the fatal flaws paid off for those 11 leaders, who now ranked in the 50th percentile. This gain of 30 percentile points essentially moved them from what most would define as being in a poor performance category to being in the category of good performance.

The average improvement for other leaders who made positive change was 22 percentile points. Those who worked to fix their fatal flaws obviously had more room to grow, while those who started at much higher levels had less room. Nevertheless, those with fatal flaws made a more substantial gain even if they didn't attain the higher levels reached by their peers. Subordinates, colleagues, and bosses were obviously impressed. Their progress was notable and appreciated by others.

On the other hand, leaders who attempt to lead while harboring a fatal flaw are like ships that try to move forward while dragging an anchor on the seafloor. Once the anchor is lifted, their progress improves greatly. Once again, this study reinforces the benefits and limitations of working on weaknesses. Fixing fatal flaws is necessary and important, and it helps a leader transition from poor to good, but the transition from being perceived as good to being seen as exceptional requires strength building.

When Do Fatal Flaws Occur

Some people might think that fatal flaws occur when leaders are young and inexperienced. They assume that as leaders gain experience, they will no longer be plagued with the challenge of possessing fatal flaws. Unfortunately this is not true. Frequently leaders get moved or promoted into a new job where a competency that was not critical in the past becomes essential in their new position. Again, we define a fatal flaw as a competency in which you receive:

- Strong negative feedback results (or poor performance review results)

or

- Below-average capability in an area that is mission-critical to your job

Being below average basically means that you perform this competency reasonably well and that it may not even be considered a weakness. However, when it becomes the centerpiece of a new job, it can now be a serious problem. When a competency is mission-critical, average performance is never good enough. Most people can think of a person who performed well at some point in his or her career only to be promoted to a position where the performance was considered inadequate. This phenomenon has been labeled the *Peter principle*. It was formulated by Dr. Laurence J. Peter and Raymond Hull in their 1969 book, *The Peter Principle*.[1] The principle states that people are promoted until they finally get elevated to a position in which they are fundamentally incompetent. They then tend to stay in that position. The book suggested that this was the explanation for why so many managers were seen as being poor leaders.

Leaving aside the obvious tongue-in-cheek levity of the book, it explains why fatal flaws often appear later in people's careers, as they are promoted to more senior positions. Behaviors that were formerly not important suddenly have the searchlight turned on them and make it appear that the fatal flaw is something new. We know that this does not need to be a permanent condition. As the above study demonstrates, leaders can fix fatal flaws and move from perceptions of being incompetent to being perceived as competent.

How to Fix a Fatal Flaw

Fatal flaws are not easy to change, but improvement is possible; and as we have previously shown, the improvement will have a substantial impact. There are a series of steps that increase the probability of improvement.

Step 1. Acceptance

The first and most necessary step is for people to accept the fact that they have a fatal flaw and that this flaw will eventually be fatal to their career if it has not already held them back. It obviously will not kill them physically, but it can permanently damage their career, negatively impact important relationships, inhibit promotions, and reduce the probability of personal success.

Until a person acknowledges the fact that there is significant negative impact that comes from the fatal flaw, nothing will change. This need to acknowledge the problem is very similar to what's required of people ready to confront alcoholism or drug dependence. The starting point for recovering alcoholics and drug addicts is to acknowledge that they have a problem.

One of the frequent dynamics of alcoholism and drug dependence is that often there are people who tend to be codependent. These are people that in many ways reward and reinforce the problem behavior. For alcoholics, these may be their drinking buddies or a spouse. With alcoholism and drug dependence, the solution is to involve those who are codependent to assist with the cure. This is also the case with people attempting to fix fatal flaws. They need to ask for and get the assistance of others in order to successfully make a positive change.

Step 2. Understand the Behavior

In order for people to change, they need to identify the problem behavior and then study the triggers that cause it to occur. If people can identify when the problem behavior occurs and what prompts the behavior, they can start to understand it better and ultimately correct it. It is important that people identify the events or stimulus that causes the behavior (e.g., "When I get in this kind of a situation with these stresses, I act out").

It is also helpful to understand the part that attitudes and beliefs play in the behavior. Several years ago we were working with a leader who got very negative scores on his ability to recognize and praise others. When we asked about his feelings toward recognition, he replied, "Only the weak need recognition." As we explored his attitudes about recognition, he explained that he was brought up in a household where his parents taught him that truly great people do things regardless of whether they are recognized or rewarded for their behavior. "You should do it simply because it's the right thing to do," he had been taught, and there was no need for recognition. As we explored this belief, we asked if it were possible that his parents were wrong about never praising good works. We then asked him how his current family felt about the belief. "They don't like it!" he proclaimed. We persuaded him that it was time to move on and try a different philosophy of recognition.

Step 3. Create and Make Measurable a Plan for Change

Once people understand a problem sufficiently, the next step is to formulate a plan for change. This plan needs to lay out goals and activities that will demonstrate a significant change to others. One of the major failings in generating a plan is that people start with a general notion of change, but in order for the change to occur, it needs to become very specific. A general notion of change might be something like, "To fix my fatal flaw, I am going to be nicer." Being nicer is a good start, but it is general to the point of being somewhat meaningless. What *specifically* does this mean?

The late Gene Dalton, a friend and colleague of the authors, identified this as one of the critical factors in a change process.[2] Plans need to move from a general notion of change to a very specific plan for change. In order for a change plan to be successful, people need to specify what they will do differently in the future, where this will be done, when it will be accomplished, and how they will go about the change effort.

Another critical factor in the change goal is to make it measurable. Keeping a tally of the number of times a person engages in the negative behavior every week is a useful measure.

Step 4. Apologize and Ask for Forgiveness

When appropriate, people may need to ask for the forgiveness of others in order for other people to accept that the change is occurring. Asking others for their forgiveness can be an extremely positive step in the change process. Asking forgiveness not only allows others to forgive and forget but also creates a higher level of accountability for the person making the change.

Step 5. Enlist the Help of Others

Many times people work on improving fatal flaws without telling others of their plans or asking for their help. Sometimes people are embarrassed by the fatal flaw, and so telling others they are working on changing and asking for their assistance is an act of humility they are not willing to take. The reality is that everyone is already well aware of the problem. This is not a big secret, and by enlisting the assistance of others, the person attempting to change will feel the support and be able to take advantage of the good ideas shared by others.

It is always interesting to tell your spouse, partner, or close friend about a change you are trying to make. They tend to remember that you are changing and remind you about those times that you slip. This can be a great benefit for a person trying hard to fix a fatal flaw.

Step 6. Reward Progress

An important aspect of the change process that is often overlooked is to find a way to reward yourself for progress and the achievement of a goal. While just making the change is rewarding in its own right, identifying a reward for yourself when a goal has been achieved can be an excellent way to keep progress on track.

The Steve Jobs Case

Steve Jobs was recognized as being an exceptional leader at Apple Computer. It was his vision that led the organization to create the Macintosh computer with its advanced graphical interface, and later the iPhone and iPad. These devices spawned the creation of over a half-million apps. Apple then transformed the music industry through iTunes. At the time this book is being written, Apple has the largest market capitalization of any company in the world. The stock price and accomplishments of this company are truly a landmark achievement.

Jobs was a hard-driving leader who was very effective at setting seemingly impossible stretch goals and targets that somehow people were able to accomplish. He had an ability to communicate in a way that generated great excitement about new products. He had a depth of knowledge in technology and a passion for design that focused the organization to create leading-edge products with exceptional form and function. He had very high standards and was willing to take the initiative to do difficult tasks.

But at the same time, Steve Jobs was often described as extremely arrogant, selfish, cruel, and nearly impossible to work with. When engineers would show him a paper with new code they had just written, he would rip up the paper, throw it at them, and tell them it was garbage. When asked why he did that, he replied that he knew they could do it better. He would criticize others in front of teammates and then a short time later would praise and reward the same people. His direct reports recalled that he would treat them like royalty one day and like the lowest form of life on earth on the day following.

Jobs was a member of an extremely small group of leaders who combine both profound strengths and what would appear to be fatal flaws. Looking at one database of over 27,000 leaders, we found only 35 leaders who had five or more profound strengths and one or more fatal flaws. They represent 0.1 percent of the population. Had they only had five or more strengths, we would predict that this group of leaders would be at the 93rd percentile on overall leadership effectiveness. But given the combination of profound strengths and fatal flaws, the average leadership effectiveness rating fell to the 80th percentile. The fatal flaw caused them to take a 13 percentile point hit on their leadership effectiveness rating. Other leaders with five profound strengths had an employee commitment-satisfaction rating at the 73rd percentile, whereas this group's rating was at the 62nd percentile.

There are two ways to look at this combination of profound strengths and fatal flaws. Some people see the data and the impact of these leaders and conclude, "It is possible to get away with having fatal flaws if you are really extraordinary at several other competencies." "Yes, the fatal flaw did take a toll on their leadership effectiveness and employee commitment scores, but it did not devastate them."

The other perspective on this extremely small and unique group is to wonder how much more effective they could have been if they had fixed their flaws. These are great leaders, but fatal flaws take a toll, they create friction, and they are an anchor that the person is dragging. We strongly recommend, even for the leader with five profound strengths, fix your fatal flaws. We believe Steve Jobs's success came, not because of, but despite his difficult behavior. We'll never know how exceptional he could have been had he chosen to change his negative behavior.

Can Strengths Be Taken Too Far?

Addressing a Common Misperception

Is There Such a Thing as a Behavior Practiced to Excess?

Yes, we think so. Chances are we can all think of some behaviors that when done in moderation are positive, but when done to excess cease to be helpful. One of the authors cites an example in his family. His wife is a wonderful organizer. Closets and cupboards are always orderly. Refrigerator shelves are labeled. Yet she is the first to admit that this can get out of hand. While cooking, she sometimes becomes more interested in reorganizing the drawer of utensils than in the meal she is fixing—and that can have unfortunate consequences. We suspect most of us can agree that there are many behaviors that can be carried to an excess, just as drinking a moderate amount of water is good for your health, while drinking multiple gallons at once can be deadly.

Can Strengths Be Taken Too Far?

A commonly held belief is that strengths taken too far cease to be strengths and become liabilities or weaknesses. Examples of that belief abound. That point of view was strongly advanced by two respected researchers, Kaiser and Kaplan, in an article in the *Harvard Business Review* entitled "Stop Overdoing Your Strengths."[1] The conclusion from this article was that people should stop working on these behaviors that *had been* a strength. In other words, back off. For example, Kaplan and Kaiser divided leadership behavior into two buckets. They labeled one group of behaviors as "forceful" and the other group of behaviors as "enabling." Each of these is defined, then, as a "strength." They observe that if a leader overuses the forceful strength by being exceedingly directive, always taking charge, making every decision, and constantly pushing people, the leader's effectiveness diminishes. That is a conclusion that we suspect most would accept. Similarly, they observe that a leader who is too cautious, gentle, understanding, mild mannered, only expressing appreciation, not standing up for personal beliefs, and being almost exclusively focused on others, will also be less effective. We would agree with that conclusion as well.

The Opposite View

We, on the other hand, also take an entirely opposite point of view. We think it is terribly confusing to tell people to work on a strength but to always be monitoring themselves to determine when they become too effective or use the strength too much. In attempting to determine why we come to such differing conclusions, we believe it starts with how we have defined *strengths*. Recall that Kaiser and Kaplan used *forceful behavior* or *enabling behavior* as examples of strengths.

However, we do not think that these fit the usual or classic definition of strengths. Indeed, we see being forceful or enabling as behavioral tactics, not strengths. These are more akin to qualities measured by a personality test or other psychometric instrument.

Strengths Defined

It may help you to review our earlier definition of strengths. It would include characteristics such as:

1. A trait that is practiced at an extremely high level, typical of the top 10 or 20 percent of leaders in a given population

2. A trait that is broadly used in a variety of situations or settings

3. At trait that is consistently used, not sporadically

4. A behavior that lasts over time

5. A trait that consistently produces positive outcomes

6. A trait that is valued for its inner worth, along with its outcomes

7. A trait that spans cultures

8. A trait that is harmonious with other strengths, rather than being opposed to them

If you apply these characteristics of strengths to *forceful* and *enabling*, you begin to see why we come to different conclusions. Let's look at *forceful*. Being increasingly forceful is seldom a positive thing. Further, being forceful cannot be effective in all situations. It does not produce positive outcomes with consistency. Being forceful is not valued for its intrinsic worth, like honesty or truthfulness would be. Indeed, some cultures are offended by forcefulness. Finally, being forceful and enabling are competing behaviors. Using one tactic more of the time means you are not doing the other.

A similar analysis can be done with *enabling*. Done to excess, it becomes less effective. And it doesn't always produce good outcomes, it is not valued for its own worth, nor is it valued in every culture; in addition, it is opposed to other strengths.

Our Research on Leadership Strengths

As noted earlier in the book, our original determination of strengths came from analyzing data on 20,000 managers, who in turn were evaluated by 200,000 colleagues. We identified 16 competencies that described the most effective leaders and distinguished them from average and poor leaders. These strengths included qualities such as:

Character and integrity

Problem-solving skills

Technical competence

Innovation

Initiative

Communication

Strategic thinking

We cannot envision many situations where doing less of any one of them would be better than doing more. Can someone be too honest? Too skilled at solving problems? Can a person be too technically competent or innovative?

Indeed, in all our data analysis, we found no evidence that extremely high scores ever had negative consequences. If that theory were true, then someone scoring at the 90th percentile would be perceived as being less effective than someone at the 60th or 70th percentile. The extremely high scorer's business results would be inferior to the results of the people who received lower scores. People would presumably be making more negative written comments about high scorers in their 360 reports than they would for those with moderate scores.

We can state unequivocally that none of the above ever happens. To the contrary, those with the lowest scores on these receive multiple negative comments and produce inferior results. Those with the highest scores produce the best outcomes on everything we have been able to measure.

Our research is quite clear about the impact of serious weaknesses, or as we have chosen to call them, fatal flaws. With rare exception, effective leaders cannot be terrible at anything. Having scores in the bottom decile (10 percent) most often sinks a leader to the lowest rungs of effectiveness.

Should You Moderate or Maximize Strengths?

Kaplan and Kaiser support the idea that backing off strengths is the right solution. They apply this solution to their definition of strengths, and they suggest that the person seen as "too forceful" should become more moderate. The "too enabling" person should be less empowering or less sensitive to others.

Our analysis confirms that exceptional leaders are those who possess three or more strengths. Our operational definition of a strength is a competency at the 90th percentile or higher. The more strengths a leader possesses, the greater the likelihood of making a profound contribution to the organization.

One executive who sought to optimize his strengths decided he wished to be more inspiring and motivating. His resolve was to do the following, and he put sticky notes on his computer screen to remind him of the following:

- Be more effusive with praise.
- Let people figure things out for themselves.
- Always ask, "What do you think?"
- Delegate more things (ask others what they'd like to do).
- Deliberately set stretch goals with my team.
- Paint (and repaint) a compelling vision.

Conclusion

In short, we find no evidence that what we and others have identified as strengths can ever be overdone. Therefore, we can't envision a time when we would advise leaders to tone down one of their strengths. Some might see these theoretical differences as subtle nuances. They are not. These result in very different approaches to improving leadership behavior.

Building Strengths with Multi-Rater Feedback

Why 360-Degree Assessments Can Be Your Best Tool

We are convinced that the single most powerful tool to help leaders identify their strengths is a 360-degree feedback instrument. While we applaud the self-assessment instruments that are available, we have rather compelling evidence that self-perceptions are not terribly accurate, and that seems to hold true for those that measure strengths or weaknesses. Having candid observations from those who work with you is an extremely helpful way to get the best possible assessment.

Then, having once discovered your strengths, the bigger and more important task is to develop them. Again, we think that the multi-rater, or 360-degree, feedback process is unparalleled in its ability to provide a comprehensive and yet granular way to help in the development process. Because the 360 instrument is so valuable in both these tasks, we have chosen to conclude this book by offering some observations about the 360-degree feedback process, suggesting how organizations can assess the quality of the instrument they are using, and we also address some of the criticisms of it.

1. Select the Correct Competencies to Measure

There are three basic ways that organizations go about developing a competency model and thereby choosing which competencies to measure with a 360-degree feedback instrument.

The first is an opinion-gathering strategy. This involves assembling a group of key leaders in the organization and soliciting from them their views about what makes an effective leader in their organization. This is often done by merely interviewing a group of corporate leaders. They are asked, "So what do you think makes a good leader in our organization?" Each person weighs in and summarizes a personal view of what good leaders know and do. In general, these comments seem to summarize the qualities that the executive believes defines his or her success.

The second method is to ask the executives to use a deck of cards. Each card describes a different competency. Leaders sort the cards into piles, thus forcing a ranking of the dozens of possible competencies.

Both of the above techniques have the advantage of obtaining the executives' commitment and buy-in, due to their involvement. The downside is that both techniques rely on the executives' knowledge of the skills required for someone in various leadership positions that may be several levels beneath them and in different functional areas. Consistency or reliability between raters is often not high. Seniority and rank can easily become dominant forces in the decision process. The competency selections are based on the feelings, intuitions, and experiences of the particular executives involved, rather than carefully collected observations and data. Many of those inputs are unrelated to the process and objective of creating a model that accurately describes the highest-performing leaders.

The third approach is to select a group of leaders and administer to them a 360-degree feedback instrument that contains a rather complete set of questions. Next, identify those leaders who are the highest performers and separate them from the average or low performers. Empirically determine, using well-established statistical techniques, which of the competencies best separates these two groups. The role of emotion is minimized. Rank, seniority, and dominant behavior give way to an empirical methodology.

We strongly favor this latter approach because of its rigor and lack of reliance on the pooled opinions of executives. This approach creates a competency model in which everyone in the organization can have stronger reliance. Because it is empirically derived, it will be more stable and less subject to being changed because a new HR vice president is hired. Scientific rigor supplants politics and opinion.

2. Show Participants How They Compare with a High Standard, Not the Average

Earlier evidence presented in this book has shown the enormous difference between the top group of performers and those who are average. Inspiring leaders don't stand before the assembled troops and declare, "I want you to be just a little above average." The better message to participants is that the organization needs them to be performing like the very best. So rather than reporting data to managers that show how they compare with the mean average, why not show them how they compare with the best? Even talking about the mean average does them a huge disservice. It has the danger of inadvertently signaling that barely above average performance is acceptable. It lacks any aspirational goal, and we think it is the wrong signal to send.

3. Measure the Impact of the Leader on Business Outcomes Such as Employee Commitment

Because the 360 is administered to the subordinates or direct reports, it is possible to incorporate a mini employee survey right into the 360-degree feedback instrument. A small number of questions provide an excellent approximation of a more full-blown employee survey. It gives a separate measure of the impact of the leaders' behavior on their subordinates. The questions are phrased in such a way that they are asking about the employees' attitudes toward the organization, not about their perceptions of their leader. Thus, while the same people are being surveyed, the measures of how the leader is perceived and the measure of the employee perceptions about the organization are quite independent.

This separate stream of data provides a useful measure of how the leader is currently impacting the group. These questions can assess employee satisfaction, commitment, and confidence in the organization. These are obviously impacted by the immediate leader, but the measure is independent.

The five items that Zenger Folkman uses in its instrument have a correlation of .80 or higher with the most highly validated engagement measures in the industry. The specific statements that we ask respondents to react to are:

1. I feel confident that this organization will achieve its strategic goals.

2. My work environment is a place where people want to go the extra mile.

3. I would recommend this organization as a good place to work.

4. I rarely think about quitting my job to go to a different organization.

5. All in all, I'm satisfied with this organization as a place to work.

4. Help the Participant to Understand What the Organization Values

The 360-degree process affords the opportunity to ask the manager, peers, direct reports, and others about their perception of what a person in a specific job or position should be focused on achieving. The 360 can ask each of these groups to select a small number of competencies that would be most important for this person to possess at a high level. This information becomes valuable input as participants decide where to put their developmental time and effort.

The feedback from each of these groups gives a more diverse, comprehensive view of what is important for a person in any given position to possess. We wrote earlier about the CPO model and the critical nature of understanding and incorporating the needs of the organization when selecting a competency to develop to a profound strength. This survey feedback provides direct input on what the organization's needs are.

5. Enrich the Feedback with Questions That Elicit Valuable Written Comments

Quantitative information is extremely helpful. It is objective. However, it often paints pictures in binary terms. Missing is the subtle messages about specific behaviors that are not measured by any statistical approach. No instrument of reasonable length can cover every conceivable topic. Written comments provide color commentary. They can deal with specific behaviors that couldn't possibly be captured by the statistical data. Personalized, company-specific information can be communicated in this narrative form. Written comments provide insight that often goes to another level of helpfulness for the recipient.

6. Make the Process a Positive, Not a Negative, One

For at least two-thirds of the participants, the focus should be squarely on discovering and magnifying strengths. We come to that conclusion because our research shows that only about one-third or fewer of all leaders have significant weaknesses—weaknesses so debilitating in their jobs that they should fix them before looking at building strengths. The great joy for most participants can be the opportunity to identify and celebrate strengths. Having a clearer awareness of these strengths then enables the individual to create a process for elevating them. There is no need for this group to focus on the more negative pathway of identifying weaknesses and determining how to fix them.

One HR vice president remarked, "There is an entirely different tone in the room when the emphasis is on helping people to find their strengths and to leverage them, than when you are looking for open wounds with the intent of pouring salt water on them." Another remarked, "A strengths-based approach creates a night-and-day difference in the attitude of the participants. Instead of coming into our sessions with their paws out in front of them, and being drug into it; they come more willingly. Who doesn't want to learn about their strengths and how to get better at using them?"

For those who possess a fatal flaw, however, it is a somewhat different story. The reality of their situation is that this fault is seriously diminishing their career. It will hold them back from promotions and better assignments. It will diminish their compensation. Life will be less pleasant, and relationships will often become sour. Is it better for them to blindly continue on that path, or is it better to find a relatively safe and constructive way for them to be given that information, with the hope that it can be corrected?

The good news is that a high percentage of participants with such flaws are able to overcome them. There is no question that the process for those with such flaws often contains some initial moments of pain. Setting a broken bone may cause some momentary pain, but it is the precursor to healing correctly.

7. Ensure That the Survey Process Is Not Laborious

In software development, great programmers write "tight" code. It is carefully structured, tested, and validated. The total number of lines of code used in the application is kept to the absolute minimum required to achieve the objective. When reviewed by others in the application development world, knowledgeable peers would say that the code is elegant in its simplicity.

The same is true in the format and structure of a well-designed 360-degree survey. Some 360 surveys have 75 to 100 questions and take 45 minutes to an hour to complete. Others have approximately 50 questions, and through efficient formatting that efficiently captures responses, they can be completed in 15 to 20 minutes. The objective is to acquire sufficient assessment information from each rater to provide validated survey results, but do it in the minimum amount of time. This requires a survey and software design that is well conceived and structured. If a leader is providing feedback for a large number of subordinates, then shorter is obviously better than longer if the survey still has validity. The organization will suffer survey fatigue if the process is lengthy or cumbersome.

8. Create Reports That Are Easy to Read and Digest

Some 360-degree feedback reports are incredibly complex. Reading and interpreting the data is formidable and nonintuitive. We feel there is no justification for that. The process can be simple and engaging, and results can be graphically displayed, easy to understand, and more rapidly digested.

Critiques of the 360-Degree Feedback Process

Some critics of the 360-degree feedback process have focused on the potentially negative aspects of the 360 instrument. Here are some of the criticisms that we have heard:

1. Feedback does not always lead to change.

2. Comparison to norms is not helpful; it just makes people feel bad.

3. People are given too much information. They can't digest it all.

4. We should tell people what and how to change and not leave it to them to decide.

5. Data from 360s should be used for purposes of making decisions about promotions and future assignments. We shouldn't use the data just for development.

6. Feedback from others is not 100 percent accurate. People don't always put down what they really think.

7. Some employees use this as an opportunity to unload on their boss, because there is no accountability for what people say.

8. It should not be necessary to give 360-degree feedback. People should have the courage to tell others, face-to-face, exactly what they think.

Responses to Critics

Our response to such criticism begins with acknowledging that no instrument or tool is perfect in every situation. We would be the first to agree that there are imperfections and that the feedback is not 100 percent accurate. However, we believe a well-designed 360 survey instrument is better than anything else that has been invented so far.

Here are some quick responses to these eight rather common criticisms of the 360 process.

1. *Feedback does not always lead to change.*
   There is strong evidence that simply receiving feedback about behavior is sufficient for many people to begin to make changes. Awareness unleashes a series of actions that corrects or changes the behavior in question. Leading psychologists, such as Martin Seligman, have been able to observe behavioral change after simply giving people feedback and then stepping out of the way.

2. *Comparison to norms is not helpful; it just makes people feel bad.*
   Feedback that shows people how they compare with others is a powerful way to capture their attention. It is reality. Feedback without some context lacks meaning. How people feel about and respond to the feedback they receive is ultimately their choice. We can do a lot to provide perspective and a path toward improvement. The alternative of not providing comparative nor-

mative data seems equivalent to the so-called ostrich solution of burying your head in the sand and hoping this will all go away.

3. *People are given too much information. They can't digest it all.* After receiving feedback, the overwhelming majority wish to repeat the process a year or so later. They learn, often for the first time, how their leadership behaviors are viewed by others. They understand better how their behaviors may be impacting business results, perhaps positively and negatively. They look forward to monitoring their change. Our data show that rather than feeling overwhelmed, they seek out people to thank them and proceed to ask for even further clarification and detail.

4. *We should tell people what and how to change and not leave it to them to decide.*
It is not long after children begin to communicate that it begins to become clear that merely telling them what to do is less effective than engaging them in a process that helps them to make better decisions for themselves. Yes, there are times when a parent must give direct orders. But it is our experience that resistance to directives often escalates as children mature.

5. *Data from 360s should be used for purposes of making decisions about promotions and future assignments. We shouldn't use the data just for development.*
This is indeed a challenging issue. It is clear that the 360-degree data are highly predictive of effectiveness. A very small percentage of organizations make this kind of data available to managers. Some do it on a limited basis by passing on the three highest competencies and the three lowest, but convey no absolute numbers or percentiles to the manager or others in the hierarchy. Why don't most organizations widely share and use the 360 development data for other purposes, like performance management? Because they have learned that when the data is used for these

other purposes, it alters the raters' candor and the completeness of the feedback being offered. Extending its usage into areas outside of leadership development becomes self-defeating, as the feedback usually loses its accuracy and value.

6. *Feedback from others is not 100 percent accurate. People don't always put down what they really think.*
We agree. Depending on the culture of the organization and the personal level of confidence of the respondent, we are confident that feedback is sanitized and moderated. As years go by and organizations repeat the process, it becomes more open. As individuals mature, they are prone to join the "truth tellers" and say what they really think. Even if not completely candid and truthful, the feedback is directionally accurate and still provides useful information to the leader.

7. *Some employees use this as an opportunity to unload on their boss, because there is no accountability for what people say.*
As we move to the point where we are approaching a half-million respondents to our 360 instruments, we have been struck by the absence of people using this vehicle as a way to irresponsibly trash a boss or peer. On a rare occasion, we'll hear of some possibly inappropriate comment, but we hear of these once or twice a year at most.

8. *It should not be necessary to give 360-degree feedback. People should have the courage to tell others, face-to-face, exactly what they think.*
This is an interesting criticism. It is easy to say that there should be no prejudice, no discrimination, and no poverty in the world and that cancer should be eliminated. Personally, we would all like to see these things happen. But those are issues over which we exert only minimal influence. Until we reach that utopian state, we educate people, we encourage charitable giving, and we

create medications that help people to conquer various illnesses. The 360-degree feedback process would not be necessary in a perfect world designed by some; but until then, it seems to perform a useful role.

Conclusion

The 360-degree feedback process is not perfect. All we can do is to repeat what was said earlier. It just happens to be much better than any other technique that has been developed to help leaders grow.

Are Leaders Born or Made?

We know of no debate that has gone on longer than this simple question, "Are leaders born, or are they made?" Highly respected researchers have emphatically declared their position in favor of one side of the debate or the other.

For example, in a 2002 article "Are You Picking the Right Leaders?" in the *Harvard Business Review*, an industrial and organizational psychologist, Melvin Sorcher, and his colleague James Brant[1] wrote, "As far as executive leadership is concerned, people are relatively complete packages by the time they arrive on the corporate doorstep." Later in the article, they said, "Our experience has led us to believe that much of leadership is hardwired in people before they reach their early or mid-twenties."

According to Sorcher and Brant, not only does "leadership hardwiring" occur at a very young age; they conclude that people change little during their careers. Only those leaders hardwired for success will excel, and this is regardless of leader development programs provided by employers. Since people don't change much, Sorcher and Brant suggest employers should focus their attention on selecting the right leaders for a particular opportunity instead of trying to develop them.

On the other hand, as we noted earlier in this book, the equally esteemed professor Warren Bennis at the University of Southern California has written:

> The most dangerous leadership myth is that leaders are born—that there is a genetic factor to leadership. Myth asserts that people simply either have certain charismatic qualities or not. That's **nonsense**; in fact, the opposite is true. Leaders are made rather than born.[2]

And so the debate continues on, and we think for good reason. Why? They are both right. Possibly the question is not asked in a sufficiently precise manner. We wish it would go away, but we don't think it will until practitioners are more accurate and candid about giving a complete answer.

A More Precise Answer to the Question

In a nutshell, here's our take on the question. Utilizing fairly sophisticated research methods involving the study of "behavioral genetics" with a group of fraternal and identical twins, one researcher showed quite convincingly that about 32 percent of overall leadership skills and behavior appear to have a genetic component to them. What is the theory? We refer to Dr. Richard Arvey[3] at the National University of Singapore. He and his research team studied the question of how much genetics influenced leadership relative to environmental factors.

They studied identical and fraternal twins to gauge both genetic and environmental factors on leadership. Because all twins share a comparable family environment, this allowed the research team to assess whether there was a difference between the identical and fraternal twins that could logically be attributed to genetic influence. Their findings concluded that one-third of the difference could be attributed to genetic factors and that two-thirds was consistent for both kinds of twins—and hence due to the environment in which they were raised. The researchers' conclusion was:

> Genes have direct impact on a number of chemical, physiological, and psychological components. These components, in turn, can impact various cognitive functioning (i.e. intelligence), personality traits, interests and values, as well as physiological capacities. Years of accumulated research has shown that many of these characteristics are heavily genetically influenced and also related to leadership. . . .

Arvey goes on to state:

> Our first study was published in 2006 and involved a sample of male twins. One hundred and nineteen pairs of male identical twins were compared against 94 fraternal twin pairs. The twins were asked to indicate the number of work-related professional associations they were serving in or had served as a leader, and the positions at work that would be considered managerial or supervisory in nature ranging from supervisor on up to President. If leadership (as we have measured it) had a genetic basis, the identical twin pairs should be more similar on this variable than fraternal twins. And indeed they were. The results of the statistical analyses showed that genetic factors could account for 31% of the variation observed in the sample subjects.
>
> A repeat of that study done with groups of female fraternal and identical twins produced nearly identical results of 32% genetic influence. This leaves 68% or 69% to be accounted for by environmental factors.

Is the Interplay of Heredity and Environment the Same for Everyone?

A further insight from this research was that being raised in an abundant environment made the genetic factor less influential, whereas being raised in a more impoverished environment made the genetic component have a stronger impact.

Scott Shane[4] advocates a similar viewpoint. Genes affect one's workplace behavior, including leadership. However, he also argues that what people do in organizations is *not* solely due to environmental forces. While genes influence a person's ability as a leader, genes alone don't determine anything about a person's work-related activity. Both genetic and environmental factors influence one's workplace behavior.

As for leadership specifically, Shane references studies that assert how DNA can influence a person's attitude toward leadership, ability to lead a group, willingness to accept a leader role, and type of boss this person will become. The twins' research by Arvey is one of the studies Shane uses as evidence for the influence of genetic differences:

> Because people tend to engage in behaviors that they are good at, those with the versions of genes that predispose them to develop leadership potential are more likely to gravitate toward leadership roles. Being in these positions allows them to further develop the skills they need to be in charge and helps them to move higher up in an organization.

Shane explains, "If your genes predispose you to develop the right personality, temperament and cognitive skills to be a boss, you are going to be more likely to angle for leadership-opportunity-rich positions."

In summary, Shane doesn't conclude that leaders are primarily born with those traits. This is because researchers don't have a complete understanding of how our genes influence us as leaders. Nonetheless, Shane offers sufficient evidence to show that genes have a noticeable effect on a person's ability to lead based on personality, intelligence level, and situations in which the person finds him- or herself.

Bruce Avolio,[5] in his book *Leadership Development in Balance: Made/Born*, also takes a middle-of-the-road position, which begins with acknowledging that genetic predisposition has an influence on one's ability to lead.

But because DNA is a fixed variable, he suggests leaders focus on the development aspect since that isn't fixed. Avolio says that "leading and learning" must go hand in hand in order for people to reach their leadership potential.

One of the key elements for developing as a leader, according to Avolio, is through understanding one's life stream:

> The life stream represents events you accumulate from birth to the present that shape how you choose to influence others and yourself. Dramatic life events can force an individual to reconsider who he is, what he stands for and the model that guides his thoughts, behaviors and actions.

The reason why people say leadership is born, Avolio contends, is because they aren't familiar with a person's life stream and the impact it has had on the person's leadership development. He believes it's the accumulation of many events over time that can shape how a person develops as a leader based on the choices she's made regarding the event. The individual has little control over life events. Yet how a person engages in these experiences is what shapes her leadership development.

Avolio also cites "internal models" as having strong influence. How people interpret significant events is the same model upon which leadership development is based. For example, one person can have a model that is resistant to change, and another person's model readily embraces change. The latter could represent someone who adapts his model over time based on life experiences. Hence, for leadership development purposes, understanding one's life model is the foundation for how you make decisions and how you can best develop leadership skills.

Practical Implications of This Research

Knowing that there is some predisposition for and genetic influence on leadership potential, there is obviously a need for organizations to put serious effort on selection processes. At the same time organizations would be unwise to ignore the opportunities for growth and development, and their responsibility to help people reach their potential.

Leadership is a pattern. It starts early. It cuts across many domains, ranging from Boy Scout and Girl Scout troops, school clubs, or church groups. People who exhibit leadership in different areas of life have a strong tendency to repeat that at later times and in varied other domains.

Earlier chapters in this book presented ways by which strengths could be developed. Knowing that roughly two-thirds of leadership behavior is strongly influenced by one's environment gives us powerful incentive and a good place to emphasize development rather than relying only on selection processes.

History of the Strengths Movement

Focusing on strengths seems like a recent phenomenon triggered by popular books such as *Flow*, by Dr. Mihaly Csikszentmihalyi, and *Soar with Your Strengths*, by Dr. Don Clifton of Gallup. For the past 20 years, there has been an increasing momentum around this topic. However, the first person on record to take a strong stance regarding the topic of a strengths focus occurred nearly 50 years ago. It was the legendary Peter Drucker, who originally wrote:

> The effective executive makes strength productive. He knows that one cannot build on weakness. To achieve results, one has to use all the available strengths—the strengths of associates, the strengths of the superior, and one's own strengths. These strengths are the true opportunities. To make strength productive is the unique purpose of organization. It cannot, of course, overcome the weakness with which each of us is abundantly endowed. But it can make them irrelevant. Its task is to use the strength of each man as a building block for joint performance.[1]

While Drucker was the first to correlate strengths with effectiveness, many others have since contributed to this subject. Some, however, have been instrumental in not only helping to shape the strengths approach to effectiveness but also enabling it to become more widely accepted, particularly in the work setting. Their work will be highlighted in this chapter.

Peter Drucker—Father of Modern Management

Peter Drucker is known as the father of modern management and was one of the world's experts on management. He wrote over 30 books on management and business. He consulted and advised business organizations and public and privately held institutions as well as government agencies. He also held academic positions at both New York University and Claremont Graduate School.

Drucker had a very clear point of view about strengths and how organizations would fare better if they leveraged the strengths of their workforce. Given the executives' role in the organization, he felt it was important for them to recognize that their talent and skills were likely the initial cause for their appointment, but that if they wanted to be effective, Drucker believed, they needed to follow a certain set of practices. These were critically important. He saw his book *The Effective Executive* as being a "blueprint and practical guide to managing one's performance and achievement."

In *The Effective Executive,* a chapter was dedicated to strengths. Drucker devoted attention to "staffing from strength" and described how this was key to the success of both the leader and the organization. Selection decisions should capitalize on people's strengths and not their weaknesses. Drucker passionately explained that individuals excel at a few strengths, and executives would be wise to place folks in roles where they can make the most significant contributions with the strengths they possess, and not wish that they possessed other traits.

He acknowledged that individuals possess weaknesses, and he advised leaders that "to focus on weakness is not only foolish; it is irresponsible. It is a misuse of a human resource as what a person cannot do is a limitation and nothing else."

Drucker further advised looking at the outcomes to be gained based on a person's strengths and to reflect on "what the person can contribute" in order to maximize the impact for the organization. His formula, therefore, for overall success for the new appointee was:

1. Design the job well.
2. Make the position demanding. Stretch the person and enable the person's strengths to really stand out.
3. Determine where the person's talent lies and know the person's capabilities long before an opportunity arises.
4. Recognize that choosing strengths means tolerating weaknesses.

When executives did the above, Drucker thought that they were ensuring not only personal success, but also organizational success, and that they needed to apply this philosophy to themselves.

The focus on strengths needs to be practiced by all for organizational effectiveness, according to Drucker: "Organizations must feed the opportunities and starve the problems. Weakness only produces headaches—and the absence of weakness produces nothing."

Mihaly Csikszentmihali

Dr. Mihaly Csikszentmihalyi is professor and former department chairman of psychology at the University of Chicago. He has studied the topic of flow for over 20 years: The study of peak or optimal experiences led to his understanding of flow:

Optimal experience represents those times when people report feelings of concentration and deep enjoyment. These
investigations have revealed that what makes experience
genuinely satisfying is a state of consciousness called flow—
a state of concentration so focused that it amounts to absolute absorption in an activity. Everyone experiences flow
from time to time and will recognize its characteristics: People typically feel strong, alert, in effortless control, unself-
conscious, and at the peak of their abilities.[2]

Dr. Csikszentmihalyi writes in his book *Flow* that these *optimal
experiences* where people feel "transcendent" and lose themselves in
the moment are states that can be produced and not left to chance.

Dr. Csikszentmihalyi describes the innumerable aspects of people's
lives such as their parents, time of birth, and their size or height that
are beyond a person's control. Consequently, it's easy to see how people can conclude they have far less control over their fate in life than
they'd like. Despite the many elements that cannot be controlled, Dr.
Csikszentmihalyi maintains that these *optimal experiences* can occur
more regularly in one's life and that certain conditions produce deep
feelings of enjoyment and exhilaration.

Dr. Csikszentmihalyi believes that his research helps individuals
see illustrations of flow in the context of a framework. That way, they
can evaluate for themselves whether the information is useful in helping them have more fulfilling, happy lives. While a variety of activities
can produce positive experiences, people have to gain a better understanding for themselves about why some things are more enjoyable for
them than others. They need to arrive at a place where they are so fix-
ated on the task at hand, that it completely absorbs all their attention
and they lose awareness of time. Ultimately, people learn the pattern
for having these enriching experiences, and that is what enables people
to feel like masters of their own destiny and gives them that sense of

overall fulfillment as a state of mind. He contends that creating flow is a key strength that people can develop.

In the work setting, it helps to find ways to give work greater meaning and purpose. In doing that, the focus should be on opportunities versus challenges and constraints. This then enables people to become even more absorbed in their work and to take advantage of their strengths.

The other way to achieve flow, according to Dr. Csikszentmihalyi, is to change the job so the conditions are conducive to flow. The job can be made more gamelike and contain energizing goals or challenges to be surmounted and opportunities for immediate feedback. This can be anyone's work experience regardless of position and role within the organization.

Donald Clifton

Dr. Donald Clifton founded SRI, a management consulting firm that later acquired the Gallup Organization where he served as chairman and CEO. Years earlier as a graduate student of educational psychology at the University of Nebraska, Clifton explored the question, "What would happen if we studied what was right with people versus what's wrong with people?" Clifton and SRI Gallup continued to study "What's right with people" by conducting positive behavior and success research. Clifton cowrote a book with Paula Nelson, *Soar with Your Strengths,* in which they drew several main conclusions:[3]

1. The study of strengths creates a new theory of what people are like.

2. Maximum productivity can be gained by focusing on strengths and managing weaknesses.

3. The study of strengths leads to an understanding of the difference between good and great.

Clifton and Nelson promoted the strengths theory, contending that "every person can do one thing better than any other 10,000 people" and noting that focusing on key strengths is the way to excellence.

They defined strengths as (1) those things a person does well and (2) a pattern of behavior that yields personal satisfaction along with other positive results.

Their formula for detecting and developing strengths included:

1. Listen to yearnings as a way to discover interests.

2. Identify activities that provide satisfaction. Where do you gain rewards? What motivates you?

3. Find easy-to-learn activities. You are likely to be good at something you grasp quickly.

4. Notice glimpses of excellence. Observe what people do well when performing at their peak.

5. Analyze excellent performance by seeing the total "flow of behavior" where the behavior comes effortlessly.

Their solution for dealing with weakness was very simple. People should "find out what they don't do well and stop doing it." But this was not referring to everything a person doesn't do well, just the things that impede productivity and self-confidence. They advised that weaknesses were to be managed because people can't turn them into strengths. Managing weaknesses enabled people to focus on building their strengths.

Clifton and Nelson were the first to suggest that the actual ratio of strengths to nonstrengths is 1:1,000, which explained why emphasizing weakness would be a huge waste of time. This helps to explain their focus on discovering that relatively small number of strengths that each person possesses. Culturally we are conditioned to improve our weaknesses, but this preoccupation with fixing weaknesses should be ignored in favor of focusing on strengths until weaknesses become irrelevant.

Martin Seligman

Dr. Martin Seligman established the Positive Psychology Center at the University of Pennsylvania, where he is also a professor of psychology. He was elected president of the American Psychological Association and in his inaugural address as he reflected on the fact that he was constantly being asked to review papers for publication in psychological journals and that they were dominated by a focus on the dark side of human nature. They were mostly on topics such as suicide, rape, depression, incest, and sociopathic behavior. He asked his colleagues why they were all ignoring success, joy, happiness, and the positive side of human nature. Seligman was an early proponent of positive psychology, which includes the study of positive emotion, positive character traits, and positive institutions; and, in fact, he is known as the father of positive psychology.

Seligman acknowledges that traditional psychology has been successful in helping people to both feel and be less sick. While that is a significant accomplishment, Seligman notes that people want more than just relief. They want to have fulfilling lives and ultimately to be happy.

He notes that there is a prevalent view, based on Freudian psychology, that maintains that people don't experience lasting happiness. Any happiness experienced is superficial and unauthentic. Seligman dismisses that argument and maintains there's no evidence to support the idea that genuine accomplishments and contributions are driven from negative motivation. Yet Freud's philosophy continues to strongly influence psychology and psychiatry, as patients examine their past for negative urges and influences. This is intended to help them understand how their experiences have shaped them into the person they've become.

Seligman distinguishes between strengths (moral) and talents (nonmoral). Strengths represent integrity, valor, and originality, whereas talents are more innate: either you have them, or you don't. One can incrementally build on talents to make small improvements. Strengths, unlike talents, can be built on and expanded, and the person needs to make choices about building a strength further and the best ways for doing so: "A strength is a trait, a psychological characteristic that can be seen across different situations and over time. A strength produces good consequences."[4]

Seligman says authentic happiness comes when people identify and build "fundamental" strengths and use them in all aspects of their life. He devised a list of strengths that individuals can potentially possess. With the help of a self-assessment, people can discover their "signature strengths." According to Seligman, authentic happiness occurs when people are able to use their signature strengths in the majority of their daily life.

David Cooperrider

> Appreciative Inquiry (AI) is about the search for the best in people and the organizations they inhabit. It focuses on the discovery of what gives "life" to a living system. It analyzes what makes organizations vibrant and effective. AI teaches how to ask questions that strengthen a system's capacity to capture and heighten organizational effectiveness.[5]

This stands in contrast to much of traditional management consulting that is focused on identifying weaknesses and threats. The big questions have often been, "What's wrong?" "How can we fix that?" In contrast, AI asks, "What's right?" "How can we magnify that?"

Cooperrider and his coauthor, Whitney, posit the question, "What would happen if all change initiatives began with a positive presumption rather than discovering a problem to be solved?" It is through the exploration of such in-depth questions that systems can grow and an optimum state be achieved.

Their quest is a dramatic switch from searching for what holds an organization back to identifying what gives "life to the system."

Relationships thrive when there is appreciation: "People see the best in one another when they share dreams . . . and when they are connected."

Conclusion

While some would assume that the focus on strengths is something of recent origin, possibly in the past 20 years, we have chronicled the strong roots that were well planted long before that. Several independent streams of research and thinking exist on this general theme. They are coming together and fortunately provide a solid empirical and theoretical basis for our modern-day focus on strengths.

We believe that our contributions to this collection of massive granite blocks that make up the current foundation of the strengths movement are the following:

1. A more rigorous analysis of the impact of strengths on business outcomes. This had not been the focus of the pioneers cited above.

2. Studies confirming that strengths can be developed, in contrast to those who believe that they are somewhat fixed or static

3. Research that confirms that developing strengths is far more successful than developing weaknesses

4. Research showing that the approach one uses to build strengths is radically different from that used to fix weaknesses. Utilizing a nonlinear approach and companion competencies makes it possible for people to move from good performance to great.

Notes

CHAPTER 1

1. Anthony J. Rucci, Steven P. Kim, and Richard T. Quinn, "The Employee-Customer-Profit Chain at Sears," *Harvard Business Review*, January–February 1998, pp. 82–98.

CHAPTER 2

1. See the work of Martin Seligman in *Authentic Happiness* (New York: Free Press, 2011) and *Flourish* (New York: Free Press, 2002).

CHAPTER 4

1. Jeff Dyer, Harold Greggerson, and Clayton Christiensen, *The Innovator's DNA: Mastering the Five Skills of Disruptive Innovators* (Boston: Harvard Business School Press, 2011).

CHAPTER 7

1. John H. Zenger and Kathleen Stinnett, *The Extraordinary Coach* (New York: McGraw-Hill, 2010).

CHAPTER 9

1. Frederick Herzberg, *Work and the Nature of Man* (New York: Thomas Y. Crowell, 1969).
2. J. M. Berg, J. E. Dutton, and A. Wrzesniewski, *What Is Job Crafting and Why Does It Matter?* (Ann Arbor: University of Michigan, 2007).

CHAPTER 11

1. J. Wilding and E. Valentine, *Superior Memory* (Hove, East Sussex: Psychology Press, 1997).
2. K. A. Ericsson and N. Charness, "Expert Performance: Its Structure and Acquisition," *American Psychologist*, vol. 49, no. 8, 1994, pp. 725–747.

CHAPTER 12

1. Laurence J. Peter and Raymond Hull, *The Peter Principle: Why Things Always Go Wrong* (New York: William Morrow, 1969).
2. Gene W. Dalton, Louis B. Barnes, and Abraham Zaleznik, *The Distribution of Authority in Formal Organizations* (Boston: MIT Press, 1973).

CHAPTER 13

1. R. E. Kaplan and R. B. Kaiser, "Stop Overdoing Your Strengths," *Harvard Business Review*, vol. 87, no. 2, 2009, pp. 100–103.

APPENDIX A

1. Melvin Sorcher and James Brant, "Are You Picking the Right Leaders," *Harvard Business Review*, February 2002.
2. Warren Bennis, *On Becoming a Leader* (New York: Perseus Books, 1989).
3. Richard Arvey, "Leadership: Is It in the Genes?" *Developing Leaders: Executive Education in Practice*, no. 3, 2011.
4. Scott Shane, *Born Entrepreneurs, Born Leaders: How Your Genes Affect Your Work Life* (Oxford: Oxford University Press, 2010).
5. Bruce Avolio, *Leadership Development in Balance: Made/Born* (Mahwah, NJ: Lawrence Erlbaum Associates, 2005).

APPENDIX B

1. Peter Drucker, *The Effective Executive* (New York: Harper & Row, 1967, 2002).
2. Mihaly Csikszentmihali, *Flow: The Psychology of Optimal Experience* (New York: Harper & Row, 1990).
3. Donald Clifton and Paula Nelson, *Soar with Your Strengths* (New York: Dell Trade Paperbacks, 1992).
4. Martin Seligman, *Authentic Happiness* (New York: Free Press, 2002).
5. David Cooperrider and Diana Whitney, *Appreciative Inquiry: A Positive Revolution in Change* (San Francisco: Berrett-Koehler, 2005).

Index

About the Authors

John H. (Jack) Zenger, D.B.A.

 John H. (Jack) Zenger is the cofounder and CEO of Zenger Folkman. He is considered a world expert in the field of leadership development and is a highly respected and sought after speaker, consultant, and executive coach.

In 2011, Jack was honored with the American Society of Training and Development's Lifetime Achievement in Workplace Learning and Performance Award. Because of his contributions to the field of leadership development and training, Jack was inducted into the Human Resources Development Hall of Fame. His colleagues in the training industry awarded him the Thought Leadership Award in 2007.

He received a doctorate in business administration from the University of Southern California, an MBA from UCLA, and a bachelor's degree in psychology from Brigham Young University. Jack has authored or coauthored 50 articles on leadership, productivity, e-learning, training, and measurement. He is the coauthor of several books, including five on the topic of leadership: *Results-Based Leadership* (Harvard Business School Press, 1999), voted by SHRM as the Best Business Book in the year 2000; the bestselling *The Extraordinary Leader: Turning Good Managers into Great Leaders* (McGraw-Hill, 2002); *Handbook for Leaders* (McGraw-Hill, 2004); *The Inspiring Leader: Unlocking the Secrets of How Extraordinary Leaders Motivate* (McGraw-Hill, 2009); and *The Extraordinary Coach: How the Best Leaders Help Others Grow* (McGraw-Hill, 2010).

He and his wife, Holly, reside in Midway, Utah.

Joseph R. Folkman, Ph.D.

Joe Folkman is cofounder and president of Zenger Folkman. He is a respected authority on assessment and change, and an acclaimed keynote speaker at conferences and seminars the world over. His topics focus on a variety of subjects related to leadership, feedback and individual and organizational change.

As one of the nation's renowned psychometricians, his expertise focuses on survey research and change management. He has more than 30 years of experience consulting with some of the world's most prestigious organizations. His unique measurement tools are designed utilizing a database comprised of over a half million assessments on almost 50,000 leaders. Because these tools specifically address critical business results, facilitating development and change is the main focus of measurement efforts. A distinguished expert in the field of survey design and data analysis, Joe consults with organizations large and small, public and private.

Joe's research has been published in a variety of publications, including the *Harvard Business Review*, the *Wall Street Journal's National Business Employment Weekly, Training and Development* magazine, and *Executive Excellence*.

Joe holds a doctorate in social and organizational psychology, as well as a master's in organizational behavior from Brigham Young University. He is the author or coauthor of many books, including *The Extraordinary Leader: Turning Good Managers into Great Leaders* (McGraw-Hill, 2002), *The Handbook for Leaders* (McGraw-Hill, 2004), *The Power of Feedback* (John Wiley, 2006), and *The Inspiring Leader* (McGraw-Hill, 2009).

Joe and his family reside at the base of the Wasatch Mountains in Orem, Utah.

Robert H. Sherwin, Jr.

 Bob Sherwin is the chief operating officer of Zenger Folkman. He joined the company in 2004 and has responsibility for all company operations. He is also one of the firm's senior leadership speakers, workshop facilitators, and executive coaches, working with clients and partners in the United States, Europe, the Middle East and Africa.

Bob has spent 25 years as an executive, a leader, a coach and a mentor in some of the world's largest and most successful training and development companies. In addition to being the COO at Zenger Folkman, Bob was the CEO of Kaset International, the SVP of Operations and CFO of AchieveGlobal, and the CFO of Zenger-Miller. All of these companies are globally recognized organizations dedicated to performance improvement in the areas of management, sales, and customer service. Bob was also the president of Industrial Training Zone, a groundbreaking provider of web-delivered technical training in PLC's and motion control.

Bob's business background also includes extensive experience in software and web application businesses. He is the cofounder and CEO of both FlipDog.com and WhizBang! Labs. FlipDog, an online recruiting website, was named by *PC Magazine* as one of the Best 100 sites on the web. Bob graduated from the United States Military Academy and earned an MBA from the University of Michigan.

He and his wife live in Alpine, Utah.

Barbara A. Steel

Barbara Steel is the senior vice president of leadership effectiveness for Zenger Folkman. Barbara is responsible for managing the facilitator network and the facilitator certification process for the company. She is also one of the organization's speakers, workshop facilitators, and executive coaches working with clients in the United States and abroad.

Barbara is a dynamic facilitator and is known for her engaging, energetic style. She leads all of Zenger Folkman's workshop offerings and helps executives implement changes to enhance their leadership effectiveness. Barbara often speaks at conferences and has been a recurring guest lecturer at the University of Maryland and Villa Julie College, located in Maryland.

For more than 25 years, Barbara's career has been dedicated to leadership, consulting, coaching and training. She was the vice president of human resources for Access Worldwide Communications, Inc., a firm specializing in multicultural marketing.

Just prior to joining Zenger Folkman, Barbara was a certified master trainer for Huthwaite, Inc. In this role, Barbara successfully consulted, facilitated, and coached business professionals and leaders with premier organizations such as MasterCard, IBM, Boston Scientific, and Microsoft.

Barbara attended Loyola University, where she received a BBA in management science. She got an MBA in organizational behavior from the Kellogg School of Management at Northwestern University. She also mentors and tutors young people to help them succeed in education and in their professional careers.

Barbara resides in South Florida.

About Zenger Folkman

Zenger Folkman is one of the world's premier providers of leadership research, assessment, development and implementation programs. The company is best known for its unique evidence-driven, strengths-based approach to developing extraordinary leaders and demonstrating the performance impact they have on organizations.